Britain's Best
Country Walks

COUNTRY
WALKING

BRITAIN'S BEST
COUNTRY WALKS

Materials © Emap Active Limited 2004
Compilation and cover design © Haynes Publishing 2004

First published in 2004

A catalogue record for this book is available from
the British Library

ISBN 1 84425 162 4

Published jointly by
Haynes Publishing, Sparkford,
Yeovil, Somerset BA22 7JJ, England
Phone 01963 440635,
www.haynes.co.uk

And

Emap Active Limited,
Wentworth House, Wentworth Street,
Peterborough PE6 1DS, England
Phone 01733 213700.
www.emap.com

Produced for Haynes Publishing and Emap Active Ltd by
Black Cat Graphics, Black Cat House, Freestone Road,
St. Philips, Bristol BS2 0QN. England

Printed and bound in England by
J.H. Haynes & Co. Ltd, Sparkford

Contents

Foreword by
Jonathan Manning

They are wild and tamed, high and low, coastal and inland, and they are all fabulous walking destinations. From week-long treks to afternoon strolls, from the rugged Scottish Highlands to the chocolate-box pretty Cotswolds, from the dramatic Yorkshire Dales to the stunning Pembrokeshire Coast Path, Britain offers the enthusiastic walker a cornucopia of regions to explore on foot.

And if you can't be out there walking, delighting in new views and enjoying nature in all its beauty, the next best thing is to be admiring photographs of new walking locations and reading about them as a prelude to planning your next trip. Which is where this book comes in.

Written and photographed by Country Walking magazine's experts, we've explored, discovered, mapped and assessed many of the finest paths through this country's most beautiful landscapes. We'll bring to life areas you have never visited, and cast new light on your favourite walking destination.

We have tested the best places to eat and drink, and sampled delicious delicacies from local food producers – all in the name of research – to ensure your next walking trip is as special as it possibly could be. And we've sourced and checked all the practical information, from the maps you'll need to handy guide books, useful addresses, and recommended routes, to make your next trip as easy and smooth as it could be.

All you have to do is find a space in your diary, book the time off, lace up your boots and head out for the finest walking Britain has to offer.

The publisher would like to acknowledge the diligent efforts of Susan Voss and the staff of Emap Licensing for making this project possible.

Cream of Cornwall

Beautiful beaches, glorious gardens, fabulous food...

Words: Marianne Powell and Perry Cleveland-Peck Pictures: Matthew Roberts

Atlantic highway – Tintagel Haven on Cornwall's north shore, a place of breathtaking beauty and Arthurian mystery.

Illustration:- Steve Hall

630 Miles from Minehead, Somerset, to South Haven Point in Dorset

Cornwall has always had a unique identity. Its language and traditions set it apart from other parts of the country, even as its extraordinary beauty attracts visitors from all over the world. Ever since Brunel built the Royal Albert Bridge at Saltash in 1859, tourists have been drawn to a place that remains curiously ancient and fiercely proud of itself. But don't be fooled by outdated ideas of quaint country folk. These days it is only the courtesy around here that's old-fashioned. Cornwall is now just as famous for new

attractions such as the Eden Project as for its historical associations with King Arthur, and it is the combination of both that make the region an irresistible prospect.

One thing that has remained the same is the area's connection with the elements. To stand on a Cornish cliff with the wind blowing through your hair and hear the sound of the seabirds above the noise of the waves is to experience what it really means to be at one with nature, to feel a very real sense of awe in the face of the beauty and power of mother earth. In Cornwall, you're surrounded by reminders of this at every turn. You're never more than 16 miles from the coast. To walk in this area is to feel a sense of peace and tranquillity that no amount of fancy scented candles can buy you back in the city.

Perhaps this is why Cornwall is at the forefront of the environmental movement. "Don't it always seem to go, that you don't know what you've got 'till it's gone," sang Joni Mitchell in 1970. Cornwall seems to have recognised this earlier than most and, over the next pages, we look at the way the Cornish community is interacting with its environment, from local farmers' markets to garden havens, from the ancient cliffs to the quiet fishing villages.

Cornwall has always been an inspiration, and not just for walkers. Painters, photographers and writers have found their muses here.

Daphne du Maurier, Cornwall's most famous daughter, started her novel Frenchman's Creek with a description of the area. We hope that this is just the start of your own adventures in one of the country's greenest havens.

"When the east wind blows up Helford river the shining waters become troubled and disturbed, and the little waves beat angrily upon the sandy shores. The short seas break above the bar at ebb-tide, and the waders fly inland to the mud flats, their wings skimming the surface, and calling to one another as they go." – Daphne du Maurier.

The Lizard Peninsula

I've never been to Cornwall before, so when I hear we're going to see the Lizard, I immediately think of the zoo. It turns out, of course, that we're going to a village, named after the serpentine rock that is common to the area. I stop being disappointed by the lack of amphibians, when I realise the coast here is one of the most beautiful places I've ever seen. We walk the coastal path around the Lizard Point while the waves gently lap in the bluest stretch of sea I've seen in this country. However, the area isn't just known for its natural beauty.

On the west of the peninsula is a memorial to Marconi, who broadcast the first ever transatlantic wireless signals from the cliffs near Poldhu, showing that Cornwall has always been a curious mixture of the old and the new.

We don't make it as far as Poldhu on this occasion, as we stop transfixed by the delights of Kynance Cove. The name comes from the Cornish 'Kénans', which means an enclosed valley. We're the only walkers in the bay, so it certainly feels private as we stand alone, facing the sea. The water is quite calm now, so I can only imagine its dangerous power during a storm.

As the spring sun shines, the cove is bathed in light, and I can't think of anywhere I'd rather be in the world on a day like this.

The rock in the bay is called Asparagus Island, and remarkably it does actually grow wild asparagus. We're feeling peckish at this point, but oddly enough, no one seems keen on swimming across the bay to climb and forage. Instead, we decide to sample some of the local food in a later stage of development, so we head for a nearby farm.

Tregellast Barton has been home to the Roskilly family for more than 40 years. This multi-talented family make everything from furniture to food, although it's the latter that's on our mind right now. We try some of their deliciously rich ice cream, which is famous throughout Cornwall, and some rum and raisin fudge. "Careful," warns Rachel Roskilly, our guide.

"As the spring sun shines, the cove is bathed in light, and I can't think of anywhere I'd rather be in the world on a day like this."

Working up an appetite for a pasty on the coast path at Kynance Cove.

"It contains real rum." I have visions of staggering along the coastal path while under the influence, as I wonder how much fudge it would take to feel tipsy. I think I'm safe with just the three pieces.

On the way out, we look around the rest of the farm. I think about heading to the furniture workshop and ordering a chair – I have a great idea for a feature that involves being carried around the South West Coast Path by willing (ahem) volunteers – but Matthew and Perry manage to drag me away before I put my plan into action. Logosen Vras! (that's Cornish for 'rats!').

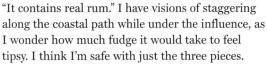

"I have visions of staggering along the coastal path while under the influence...   ...of rum and raisin fudge!"

The Route

The Lizard

Distance: *10km/6¼ miles*
Start: *Park near the Lizard lighthouse (grid ref SW703117). Follow the road down towards Polpeor Cove then turn right on to the South West Coast Path. Follow the trail along the cliff path, passing through Kynance Cove. When you reach Soap Rock (grid ref SW677144), take the footpath inland and then make a right turn to go south. At the fork in the footpath, continue inland towards Chapel Lane and enter Lizard on this path. Follow the road down back to the car park.*

The Eden Project

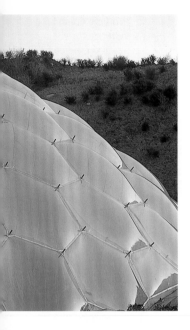

"Eden isn't so much a destination as a place in the heart...a statement of our passionate belief in an optimistic future for mankind."
– Tim Smit, founder of The Eden Project

Cornwall is at the cutting edge of new environmental practice and attractions. The futuristic biomes of The Eden Project have become an iconic symbol of the area's regeneration and inventiveness. This modern project attracts visitors from all over the world, just as the legends of old have drawn tourists to the region for generations. The project is just a hop, skip and a jump from the South West Coast Path, and is well worth the diversion. And, in keeping with sound environmental principles, entry is cheaper if you make it there without a car. There are good networks of footpaths in the area, and plans are afoot to create a direct footpath between the project and the nearest railway station, at Par.

Once inside, you'll find an amazing variety of plants from around the world, grown within a unique environment. If you're not planning a tropical holiday this year, then a quick trip to the humid zone will let you live the dream for at least an hour. Simply close your eyes and let the rich smell of the plants and the humid mist transport you to a more glamorous location. If you've set your sights on a European break, try the temperate zone, where Mediterranean herbs and olive trees are dotted along the paths, a tantalising insight into living and walking on the Continent. Of course, with the delights of the Cornish Riviera at hand, you might not want to venture further afield ever again.

Inside the futuristic biomes of the Eden Project's Tropical Zone.

The Temperate Zone includes plants from the continent.

The Lost Gardens of Heligan

Day three of our Cornish caper finds us on the coast near the village of Mevagissey. After the sea air of the previous days we decide to head inland and, having casually skimmed a few pebbles across the lapping waves, we reluctantly leave the beach behind. We make our way from Mevagissey along a steep path that leads directly to the Lost Gardens of Heligan, where unexpected treats await.

When I was a child I used to love reading The Secret Garden. The idea of finding a hidden land appealed, and whenever I was out in the country I'd peer optimistically beyond high stone walls and bramble thickets in search of the real thing. I was always disappointed...until today.

Like the garden of the book, Heligan used to be a neglected space that was brought back to life with the care and attention of a new generation.

The gardens have existed since the 16th century, and reached their peak in Victorian times as the property of the wealthy Tremayne family. Then the First World War came along, taking away the team of gardeners that had maintained the grounds. The gardens started a slow process of decline until they were entirely covered with brambles. They were

long period of neglect. Out of 300 camellias, for example, 55 were planted before 1914. Other growing techniques, including the pineapple pit, have been revived. In Victorian times the squire served pineapples to show off to important guests. They might not have been so impressed to learn that it took 30 tons of fresh horse manure to rot in order to raise the temperature to grow these tropical fruits.

"The Jungle Walk is pure Indiana Jones territory, where wooden walkways and bridges intercut towering Antipodean tree ferns and exotic plants."

Generous geology, landed lobster pots, luscious lichens and shapely shore life – the bounty of the South West Coast Path.

The enchanting 'Giant's Head' at Heligan.

'rediscovered' in 1990 by Tim Smit, of Eden fame, who set about returning them to their former glory with colleague John Nelson.

"We wanted to restore the Lost Gardens as a tribute," says Tim, "not to the lords and ladies of past eras, but to the working people who had implemented their grand plans as well as routinely servicing their needs."

These days, the Lost Gardens of Heligan are rightly regarded as the eighth wonder of the world, and offer a treasure trove of unusual flora to wonder at as you wander – you'll probably stay at strolling pace because there's so much to look at. There are three miles of walks around the various sections, and although it might not sound much, be prepared to spend a full day here if you want to appreciate fully the amazing variety of the grounds.

A remarkable number of plants have survived the

Attractions for walkers range from leafy woodlands to jungle trails, where a micro-climate ensures the temperature is about five degrees Celsius higher than the rest of the gardens. The Jungle Walk is pure Indiana Jones territory, where wooden walkways and bridges intercut towering Antipodean tree ferns and exotic plants, including skunk cabbage, which fortunately doesn't smell as bad as the name would suggest. The backdrop of magnolias and rhododendrons complements the giant rhubarb plants, which would need several vats of custard to cover them. The banana plantation bravely withstands the Cornish winters, while the bamboo tunnel was created by necessity from the overgrown Japanese garden.

With such a profusion of plant life, it's no wonder that Cornwall is challenging Kent for the title of 'Garden of England'.

The Route

To Heligan and back
Distance: *7.2km/4 1/2 miles*
Start: *Park at the Heligan Gardens (grid ref SW001466). When you've finished exploring, take the footpath from the bottom of the grounds towards Mevagissey. When you reach the town, head for the South West Coast Path and follow it north to Barton Farm (grid ref SW016474). Bear left to cut across the road on to the footpath back to Heligan.*

Tintagel

There is one individual who perhaps personifies the British countryside more than any other. He is, of course, that legendary figure of the round table, King Arthur, whose story is the story of these, our own islands. From the Peak District to the Sussex Downs, Arthur's name has long been linked to the many mystical places of our lands, but no more so than at Tintagel in Cornwall, where Arthur was said to have been brought into this world.

Today, we are walking in the footsteps of this ancient king of England. Legend has it that Arthur's father, Uther Pendragon, fell in love with the beautiful – already-married – Igraine of Tintagel and asked the wizard Merlin to magic him into Igraine's Cornish home so that he might seduce her. Merlin agreed, Uther met Igraine in her room, and Arthur was conceived.

As we approach this celebrated place from Trebarwith Strand to the south, the salty Atlantic winds seemingly bent on keeping us from our chosen course, it seems we are indeed walking some bewitched path. A pair of screeching buzzards hunt for prey along the cliff edge to our left, ancient tumuli lend peculiar undulations to the grassy fields ahead, out in the bay Gull Rock shape-shifts before our eyes as we twist and turn along the coast.

Today, this 'Atlantic road' stretch of the South West Coast Path seems bleak and uninviting, a mirror image of the warmth of Kynance Cove we so enjoyed yesterday. It is a place where you must walk with vigour, a spot where man has had to struggle to survive. Between Trebarwith and Tintagel are many a disused quarry, the ubiquitous lichen-covered drystone walls en route a testament to this, and in Hole Beach stands a spectacular rock pillar, carved out by discerning quarrymen – or perhaps Arthur's twisted half-sister, Morgan La Fey. Some of the local quarries were worked within living memory, and the entrances to the square tunnels in the vertical cliff faces are still there. The work was incredibly hard. At times it took place around the tides, the day starting at four in the morning.

From the youth hostel at Dunder Hole we head inland a little to the 10th-century St Materiana's church, the oldest in Cornwall, before reaching a crest on the coast path for the views over Tintagel Head and The Island.

The Island isn't in fact an island, but a peninsula attached to the mainland by a thin and ever-eroding strip of land. What now appears to be the peculiar remains of two castles, attached by a steep and looping flight of steps, was once just one structure straddling the peninsula.

Sadly, there is no historic evidence to suggest that Arthur lived at Tintagel (though a sixth-century plate bearing the inscription 'Artognov' was found here recently). But archaeology has concluded that people were living here between the fifth and sixth centuries, Arthur's time, and a spring discovered at the top of the island certainly lends weight to the theory that Tintagel has been occupied for a long time. While the ruins of the castle you see today are certainly ancient, they were not around in Arthur's time. Today's castle was built by Earl Richard of Cornwall, younger brother of Henry III, in the 12th century.

Gravestones at Cornwall's oldest church, St Materiana's, en route to Tintagel Castle.

The rock pillar at Hole Beach.

The Route

Arthur's footsteps

Distance: *9.7km/6 miles*
Start: *Park at Trebarwith Strand (grid ref SX053864). Pick up South West Coast Path and head north to Tintagel Head, via St Materiana's (grid ref SX050885). From the castle head into the village and pick up footpath at The National Trust's Old Post Office, a 14th-century building that served the district for 50 years in the 19th century, to Trevellick Farm. Head along road to Treknow and pick up footpath back to Trebarwith Strand.*

Before you go...

STAY HERE

Tregaddra Farm near Helston offers a warm welcome to walkers. We used this working farm as a base to explore the coastline around the Lizard. June Lugg provides well-equipped rooms and a hearty breakfast for a day's walking. There are also tennis courts and a covered swimming pool.
Tregaddra Farm, Cury Cross Lanes, Helston, Cornwall TR12 7BB. Tel 01326 240235 or visit www.tregaddra.freeserve.co.uk

Bokiddick Farm (pictured) near Bodmin is remote enough to get away from it all, as well as being convenient for the north coast of Cornwall. A newly developed barn complex offers a modern, comfortable base for visitors. The Hugos are your welcoming hosts.
Bokiddick Farm, Lanivet, Bodmin, Cornwall PL30 5HP.
Tel 01208 831481 or visit www.bokiddickfarm.co.uk

VISIT HERE

The Eden Project

Location: Boldeva, St Austell.
Opening Hours: October 27th to March 24th,10am to 4.30 pm, last entry 3pm.
March 25th to October 26th, 10am to 6pm, last entry 5pm.
Open every day except Christmas Eve and Christmas Day. The humid zone is closed on February 24th and April 11th, with half-price entry on these days.

EAT HERE

Country Walking sampled produce at Roskilly's. The farm complex is open to visitors free of charge and it is possible to see ice cream, fudge and apple juice being made. The farm shop is open from 10am to 5.30pm daily between Good Friday and October. During winter months the shop opens weekends only, times vary, phone for details before setting out.
Tregellast Barton, St Keverne, Helston TR12 6NX. Tel 01326 280479.

VISIT HERE

Tintagel Castle

Location: Five miles from Camelford, signposted from the A39. Tintagel Head is half a mile from Tintagel village along an uneven track. No vehicles, so you'll need to park in the village.
Opening hours: Open daily from 10am, Closes 6pm April-September, 5pm October, 4pm November-March.
Closed December 24th to 26th, January 1st.

VISIT HERE

The Lost Gardens of Heligan

Location: Pentewan, St Austell.
Opening hours: November to March, 10am to 5pm, last entry 3.30pm. April to October, 10am to 6pm, last entry 4.30pm. Open every day except Christmas Eve and Christmas Day.

VISIT HERE

The National Maritime Museum, Discovery Quay, Falmouth

The National Maritime Museum in Falmouth has been given a dazzling multi-million pound re-design. As well as housing the country's best collection of boats, it looks at the lives of the people who built them and explores the universal appeal of setting sail. The museum is situated on the waterfront, and visitors can experience life under the sea from the safety of an underwater viewing gallery. With interactive displays and the chance to try boat crafts for yourself, this is the ideal stop-off for anyone with an interest in the open seas and marine environment.
Opening hours: 10am to 5pm daily. Open every day except Christmas Day.

Off the leash

The stepping stones at
Laughter Hole – Max takes
the lead, while Boot lingers
with Peter, host and pack
leader, and Richard.

Just you, your best friend and 368 square miles of incredible moorland. Discover why Dartmoor's limitless landscapes and beguiling trails are made for you and your dog.

Words: **Richard Baker** Pictures: **Matthew Roberts**

Ahhh, the rich pong of rabbits, the overpowering whiff of sheep and, rrruff, those wide open spaces in which to practise tail chasing with tuck, front tumble without reason, and other daft gymnastics.

All these pleasures could be your dog's if you walk on Dartmoor. Meantime, you can look forward to wonderful trails without stiles or livestock so you can let your friend off the lead, hotels and B&Bs that welcome muddy paws...and a tale. It is over 100 years since Arthur Conan Doyle wrote one of the world's most famous dog books – The Hound of the Baskervilles.

It wasn't a cheery story, but it has left its mark on Dartmoor and our collective consciousness – think of Dartmoor and, alongside the infamous prison at Princetown, you'll probably think of

that gigantic black dog howling in the mist. Sherlock Holmes finished the blighter off, but myths and legends are legion hereabouts, of packs of wild dogs, some black, some white, all with an attitude problem, intent on inflicting unspeakable harm upon you should you walk in the wrong place at the wrong time.

Of course, we think that's piffle and, to prove it, we thought we'd walk the moor in the company of our own slavering hounds. Two black and two golden Labradors, entirely capable of licking and nuzzling you to death, if cornered.

There is an incredible number of walks to choose from, but we've picked four that incite the most canine interest. Oh, and if you don't have a dog to walk with, it absolutely doesn't matter. The moor will seduce you anyway.

Walk one

Elementary, my dear Watson

"We walk at high noon, with a weak sun revealing a wonderful amphitheatre of yellowed grass."

"A long low moan, indescribably sad, swept over the moor – the Hound of the Baskervilles calling for its prey." And so, under lantern-lit pages, Arthur Conan Doyle rose Victorian hairs and goosebumps.

The great Grimpen Mire of Doyle's imaginings, lair of the Hound, is said to be based upon Foxtor Mires, a boggy, tussocky bowl south of Princetown. Doyle walked here when researching his book. In the gloaming or in mist, it's a spooky, desolate place, fractured by a lonely wall, hiding grass-topped bogs that legend, but not fact, claims will swallow a horse sideways and which, in bad weather, can lead to a hopeless loss of direction.

But we walk at high noon, with a weak sun revealing a wonderful amphitheatre of yellowed grass. Silver rain is glinting off the tumbledown enclosures of the old tin mine at Whiteworks. There are deep wells to admire where hardy moorsmen once toiled, and a shallow meandering leat, a trench dug to feed water to towns further north and east.

The dogs are loving it. Tails emerge from behind clumps of straw, paws appear on top of mossy walls, there's a spring and a Labrador leaps into the landscape. Then another, and another before Boot, with his awkward front legs, brings up the rear.

We follow waymarker posts and sheep tracks across the mire, guessing the woolly ones' nimble hooves will have forged the dryest passage across these slopes. Our goal is the hilltops, where a few black clouds smudge the skyline – the emptiness of it all is thrilling. There is no one in sight, just a few dark ponies silhouetted on the road towards Princetown.

After tip-toeing across the froth of Swincombe River, we reach Goldsmith's Cross, one of the many gaunt granite markers that guided monks across the wilderness in medieval times. Soon after, we find another cross on top of Childe's Tomb, where an errant feudal lord died alone with his steed, lost in bad weather. They like a woe betide yarn in these parts.

It's here that we rest. I lean back against the rock and sense the moor – there's a skylark chattering, tracing endless circles in the clouds. The wind is strong but silent, probably because I'm the only thing it can buffet, and there's a smell of minerals in the air, wafting up from the footfalls we've made in the boggy earth. My boots are healthily grimed and I'm pleased by that – it's no good returning spick and span to the lodgings when mud is evidence of our indomitable journey.

Max isn't so sure about this sensory break in the game. He sits close, nose twitching, mud socks reaching halfway up each leg, desperate to gambol on. Then I spot two fellow walkers on the other side of the bowl. At first I think it's dirt in my eyes, but binoculars reveal two figures scratching along, bending over every few strides. They're botanists! Or very odd. But we are no longer alone.

We walk on west along the contour, past more old mine workings, still and cold, to another ravaged cross. It's hard to imagine how ancient travellers survived here without the comfort of a Mars bar and car at the end, but that's the key to this wild walk, using the cinema in your mind to picture the past – the landscape hasn't changed, just the people.

Meanwhile, Wellie has spotted familiar ground and takes a manic lead back across tussocks to Whiteworks. Dogs and humans already have a spring in their steps, and there are three more adventures to come.

Introducing the hounds...

From left to right)
Boot: *One year, dodgy front legs slow him, but enthusiastic and an expert user of sad-eye technique*
Wellie: *Eight years, distinguished father figure who tolerates the young'uns and is fond of pork pies*
Barnaby: *One year, simple, headlong, always up for a scrap and a prolific chewer of sofas*
Max: *Eight years, inquisitive, affectionate, the chief rabbit chaser and instigator of mischief*

start/finish

Whiteworks

Whiteworks Tin Mine

Foxtor Mires

Childe's Tomb

Nun's Cross Farm

Tin Workings

Fox Tor

Crosses

N

The Route

Whiteworks and Foxtor Mires

Distance: *7km/4¼ miles*
Time: *2½ hours*
Start: *At Whiteworks (SX614711), pass mine shafts to edge of mire and follow sheep track and post on bearing south east and then south west to cross bog. Climb hill, then bear east to Childe's Tomb (SX625704) before sighting and reaching Fox Tor. Follow contour level west to Nun's Cross Farm (SX605698), then take Abbot's Way bridleway back to Princetown road and start. You need to be able to use a compass for this walk, and take care in the bogs – they may not swallow you whole, but a wrong path in poor weather will make the going hard and wet.*

Walk two Tor stories

Whirr, click – the sound of my camera out of control on the walk between Hound Tor and Haytor Rocks, probably the most famous and photographed lumps of granite on the moor. The tors have played a part in many of the 19 film versions of Sherlock Holmes' adventure, even though neither has any role in the book. Hound Tor is so-called not because it looks like, or is haunted by, a hound, but because of a corruption of its Domesday name, Hundatora.

Gaze at either rock, and bizarre silhouettes can appear – faces, monsters or, in my case, a cheeseburger with droopy lettuce leaves. Look away from their tops and you are in the heavens, with Earth rumpling, fissuring, endless before you.

And the dogs? Well, judging by the ridiculous let's-bark-at-a-boulder game the Labradors are playing, they love it here too.

This is also a trail with added oxygen. We're more than 1,000ft up in the path of trade winds that have had no landfall and no chance to pick up the miasma of spent petrol. From our first hike up to the rocks and down through the gorse on the other side, we're quickly in – and exhaling balloonfuls of concentrated O.

But it's cold, too, and I add another layer from my rucksack as we step into Hound Tor village. It lies at the sandy foot of the tor itself, and was abandoned in the 14th century, probably because of the Black Death, or perhaps because farming had become too hard – the local abbots weren't known to be generous landlords. It's become a series of low ruins, which we pick our way around, thinking but not comprehending what it must have been like to reap this soil for rye.

Next we reach the clapper bridge over Becka Brook, the great stones laid by ancient brawn. They are as sturdy now as then – when once they were used to travellers with coarse hassocks and oak staffs, today it is the rustle of Gore-Tex and the scratching of tungsten-tipped poles on their stone.

Over the bridge and we're into the relief of trees, cosily out of sight and unable to see even the tors' tops. The dogs can sniff in earnest here, the smells are concentrated and can't be blown away. Wellie roots at the base of brambles, and is excited to find half a pork pie left by an earlier explorer, but which is quickly removed from reluctant jaws by Peter. The nose clearly works, but so much for honest animal tracking.

The lower levels don't last long, however, and we greet a radiating sun head-on as we climb Black Hill. The dogs, more subdued in the shade, hurtle ahead to the road. (Traffic is light, but you may want to put your animals on a lead here – it depends how well they answer your call. The same applies when among the livestock that shuffles around Haytor.)

We're in the sky again, trying to fathom the Herculean deeds of 19th-century pick-and-shovel men. Granite rails run away to our left, built when iron was too expensive and difficult to lug this far into the moor. Max has his snout to these thick grey blocks and follows them to their source at Haytor quarries. From here teams of horses dragged rock that was used to build the British Museum and London Bridge (the one that American took home to Arizona).

Haytor is a popular stopping point for car tourists, so whichever day you walk you'll have company. We stride on, though – the ground is good and firm, the way is clear and the entire moor seems to slope downwards to the north, making our path home easy to follow. More odd shapes are juggled in the mind at Saddle Tor and then Top Tor, before Wellie, Boot, Barnaby and Max are reeled in for the short road-walk back.

"This is also a trail with added oxygen."

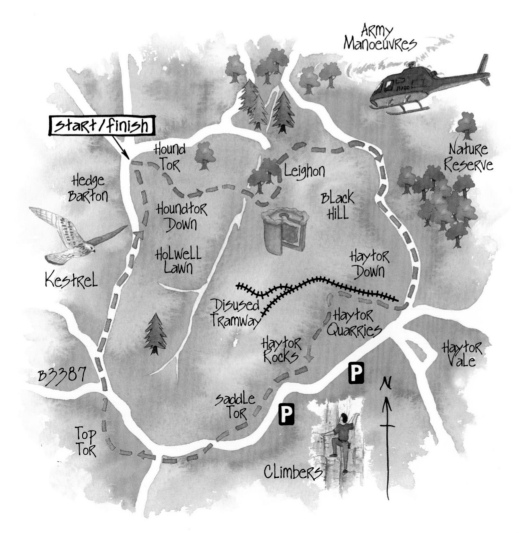

The Route

Hound Tor and Haytor Rocks

Distance: *8km/5 miles*
Time: *3 hours*
Start: *From Hound Tor car park (SX739793), explore rocks and walk on to the remains of Hound Tor village. Take bridleway east over Becka Brook clapper bridge, following path along wood edge across to Leighon. Take track north to road rising past Yarner Wood Reserve across Haytor Down to Haytor Vale village. Just before village, look for tall stone on right (SX768775) with parallel strips of stone on ground. Take tramway to fork, then left to Haytor Rocks, on to Saddle Tor to B3387. Follow road to junction, take right, then continue on road south beside Holwell Down. About 200m after crossing brook, take bridleway east into Holwell Lawn, heading north on paths to Hound Tor and your start.*

Walk three
Beware the Wisht Hounds

Dogs like to help, so Barnaby, who knows nothing at all about grid references, has just plonked his very muddy paw over the section of the map we are about to walk on. It's uncanny, because he could have put the offending print anywhere else but Wigford Down and we'd have been all right. But we forgive him.

Wigford is the source of, perhaps, the scariest fable on Dartmoor. Here, Dewer (aka the Devil) and his pack of coal-black Wisht Hounds hunt the souls of unbaptised babies and anyone else who looks lost or vulnerable. They chase their victims down from a wood near Princetown until the unfortunates are driven over the cliff of the spectacular Dewerstone, and fall to their fate on rocks by the River Plym.

Of course, much of this savagery takes place on misty nights and, because it's quite bright today, we're not scared. I think the spooky feeling tingling in my spine is down to the stone circle we're sitting in. Ancient rites and sacrifice have never made me feel very comfortable – I think because the stones represent fact, not myth, and I'm sat where a congregation once cowered.

The dogs are quiet here, too, and are content to stick muzzles in the air and peer through squinting eyes out on to the wonderful western moor, to Great Mis and Cox tors and, directly behind us, the huge dam at Burrator Reservoir.

This high ground is perfect for walkers. There's enough undulation to exercise the hamstrings, but it's firm enough underfoot to keep the going good. Only the sheep, heavily daubed in the local farmers' blue, leave offerings that test the placement of our feet.

South of the circle we descend to the Dewerstone, a mighty stanchion of rock more than 200ft high. We inch forward to its edge and peer below at the river, which is easily heard and soon spotted through the barren branches of a valley filled with old oaks. We'll be down there soon, but choose not to take the most direct route. There is an inviting path running beside the rock, but I reckon you need ropes to descend it.

We head north from the rock before zig-zagging south again, down rubbled tracks, past old quarries sunken in shrubbery and into the river gorge.

It's good to be beside water, with the mighty oak trunks rising above. Our voices and barks echo in the gorge as we raise them above the level of the Plym.

Teabreak on Wigford Down Stone Circle.
Can Barnaby sense the Wisht Hounds?

Above us the Dewer's lip of granite is more than just a limit to our walk – it's also a southerly boundary of the moor. From here the Plym gets fatter and wider until the sea, and the ground becomes lower and more fertile. As the path back to base winds high above the river's southern banks, it offers what seems like a trespasser's view into the hallowed moor. I stand on tip-toes to look back inside, but it won't do. Then, as if to rub it in, a buzzard cries above – she can see it all.

There is moisture in the air now, and this makes the trees and gorse feel closer. Spray flicks off the toes of my boots, grassy wisps cling to my trousers.

My eyes begin to water and my skin is clammy. It's strange – but exhilarating – what the slightest change in weather can do to your emotions. As we walk east we're greeted by a huge white scar on the next moortop, where an almighty trowel has scooped the heart out of the hillside. This is the blue clay works, which – good news – is due to close soon after a long-fought campaign by conservationists. It will mean less in the way of china teapots but, hopefully, even more wild land to walk on.

"Hey dogs," I call. "That'll be nice, won't it?" But my friends are weary and barely lift their eyelids. We're all happily flagging. We don't even have the decency to feel guilty about interrupting a ram and ewe's embrace as we enter the car park.

The Route

The Dewerstone and River Plym

Distance: *8km/5 miles*
Time: *2 hours*
Start: *At car park north of Cadover Bridge (SX554648) head south west on to Wigford Down. At stone cross (SX553647) follow boundary wall west for nearly a mile until semi-circle of boulders, below which is Dewerstone Rock. Head west from rock into trees, until reaching path. Go right, slightly downhill, until U-turn south west on broad path, which becomes increasingly rubbly and zig-zags down into the River Plym valley, and the crossing at Shaugh Bridge. Follow B-road signed into Shaugh Prior, but take footpath left signed for Cadover Bridge shortly after. The path climbs on to West Down and tracks the river east through North Wood over footbridge at Dunstone back to car park.*

25

Walk four
Stepping stones

The clapper bridge at Postbridge, one of the most famous sites on Dartmoor, but just try getting four dogs to pose still on it for one second.

"The East Dart is a perfect river – the flow is like polished glass, its bottom a mosaic of stones glinting gold, amber and jade."

The Route

Postbridge and Bellever
Distance: *10km/6¼ miles*
Time: *3 hours*
Start: *At Lydgate House Hotel (SX652787), follow bridleway to Pizwell and Runnage Bridge, then east beside wood. Take bridleway across Cator Common to road. Follow for 1km then take bridleway south to Sherwell, up hill through Babeny farm to stepping stones (SX663757). Follow river on east side to Bellever Bridge, east on road and then bridleway back to Postbridge and start.*

The dogs know this final walk, because it starts at their front door, so we let them show the way. As the East Dart river breaks away beside us, we march out through farmland. It's cold and a brisk pace is needed to make the veins bulge and the lungs burst into life.

With pasture, gates and stiles, a farmer spraying muck and a sheepdog yapping a greeting to his furry rivals, it's like any shires scene in Britain, except we have to ford brooks via ancient stepping stones and the cattle are shaggier than you'll find in the Home Counties.

This is Dartmoor in many guises. From the haphazard geometry of the fields we move into heather, gorse, tall pines and a sandy soil – it reminds me of the New Forest. We fall down into warm dells, past Pop Larkin farms, beside lumpen stone walls. These hurdles are filled with the mightiest slabs, each decorated with the sheen of crawling lichen.

I feel I should be leaning against them, unfolding a napkin of cheese-and-pickle doorstep sandwiches, a flagon of cider close to hand, but this is the longest of our walks, and we've no time for elevenses.

Soon we're striding across Cator Common, its thin, grassy top and firmness underfoot a relief for ankles used to picking each step through the heather. The common is home to another fearsome pooch legend, a white-fanged phantom that howls in the mist. Apparently, it's guaranteed to give you the shivers, but will do no harm.

Barnaby, who were he born another creature would have been a bull, is first down the hill and into the river near Laughter Hole. Splish, splash and out he bounds, keen to show how much fun he's having with a soaking shake in our direction. Boot follows, but has to lock the front brakes on in spectacular style as he discovers the stepping stones. As his pals pile across, leaping from one polished rock to another, Boot is left behind.

His front legs can't be trusted to land and leap again in one movement. We spend 10 minutes imploring and encouraging those sad, black eyes. He barks and fidgets in frustration, but then takes the initiative and jumps into the flow, swimming the void in seconds and clouting the odd brown trout in the process.

The East Dart is a perfect river. The flow is like polished glass, its bottom a mosaic of stones glinting gold, amber and jade. Boulders lie at pleasing intervals, creating a confusion of slacks and glides. The olive pines and high blue sky are reflected in technicolor on its surface.

The path by the river is wonderful, an open plain of soft turf, bounded by water and a hillside hiding the remnants of ancient cottages and the flotsam of the Dart in flood.

This isn't a walk of gigantic views. It's cosy and secure in a greater moor of wide open spaces. Our first sight of a horizon is near home, as we work our thighs to the top of the hill above Bellever. Far beyond is the North Moor, the White Tors, Fur Tor, Winney's Down and mysterious Grey Wethers stone circle. There are no roads there, and no houses, just endless bewitching trails for the intrepid. It's tempting, but my stomach grumbles that a pint and a pie sounds better.

On their best behaviour...

With few stiles and open access across most of the moor, you can walk your dogs freely across the unspoilt acres. But care must be taken around livestock. Dartmoor ponies are fairly docile, but near sheep your dog must be under close control. From March 1st to July 15th, extra care must be taken to avoid disturbing rare ground-nesting birds, ewes and lambs. If you are in any doubt about the behaviour of your dog, it should be kept on a lead.

Before you go...

Where to stay

Country Walking stayed at the five-star Lydgate House Hotel, near Postbridge, in the heart of the moor. Rooms are immaculately furbished, the lounge is a place where you'll want to dwell for hours, and the service and food provided by proprietors Cindy and Peter Farrington is superb. Well-behaved dogs, of course, are welcomed. Rooms start from £35 a night. Our stepping stones walk starts at the hotel's door.
Tel 01822 880209 or visit www.lydgatehouse.co.uk

Lydgate House, the start of our final walk. Good teacakes, too.

Planning

For more information call Dartmoor National Park Authority on 01822 890414 or, better still, drop into the visitor centre at Princetown for up-to-date news on weather, army firing restrictions, guided walks and all manner of useful advice. The Dartmoor Tourist Association, tel 01822 890567, provides a visitors' accommodation guide with details of B&Bs, hotels and guest houses, including those that welcome dogs, plus day attractions at sites all over the moor.

Maps

Ordnance Survey Outdoor Leisure 28 (1:25,000) covers the entire moor, as does the Harvey Dartmoor map (1:40,000), which also has useful facts for visitors.

North and South: the Downs debate

Words: **Perry Cleveland-Peck**   Pictures: **Tom Bailey**

All families share their differences of opinion. Mine is no exception. Put us all together and we row more than a coxless eight at Henley regatta. Between us we can, and do, argue about anything and everything – usually all at the same time. When it comes to walking, however, the family fuss involves just two of us.

My brother, Justin, and I have always enjoyed something of a chalk-and-cheese relationship. Don't get me wrong, he's my best friend. But if I like the Rolling Stones, Justin likes the Beatles; if I enjoy a cup of black coffee, Justin likes a sweet milky tea; if I got all the brains, Justin…well, let's not go into that.

So being brought up near the lovely Ashdown Forest in south-east England, you'd think that, mercifully, there aren't too many walking routes to argue about. Think again. For the premier, numero uno, single-most cause for friction between us involves our choice of walking location. It is known by our parents as the great

north-south divide but, being soft southerners, we're not talking about the Lake District vs the Cornish Coast, or the Peak vs Dartmoor. No, sadly and shamefully, we're not even talking about that area of wilderness north of the Dartford Tunnel. Because whereas Justin has been, and always will be, a sucker for the South Downs, I prefer to enjoy them from afar – from as far as the North Downs Way, in fact, in Surrey.

These two, often parallel, long-distance routes have long been the setting for many a friendly fracas, the one walker always looking longingly north or south while the other advances the merits of the trail they are actually on.

And so, in the spirit of hatchet burying (rather than the burying of brothers), Justin and I set out to walk the choice bits of each other's preferred ridge in the hope that you, dear reader, can resolve this fraternal dispute once and for all.

Walk South

"To our left is the aquamarine sea. To our right, an earthy reflection of the ocean itself, are the undulating waves of this chalk landscape. It is stunningly beautiful."

Beachy Head, with its stunning chalk cliffs

"Your problem," says Justin as we walk up the cliff path from Beachy Head, "is that you don't appreciate beauty when you see it." We pause for a breather, the chalk from the cliffs underfoot lending the Channel a startling peppermint colour, the wind tearing the words from our mouths. "You rush about the countryside with your notebooks and cameras, and you don't actually stop to look at what's in front of you. I mean, isn't this the most beautiful spot in the world?"

I'm half thinking of responding with some pithy comment on how I am at least fit enough not to have to stop every five seconds, but my brother does have a point. We're cresting one of the magnificent green folds of this rolling English countryside, a more quintessential Downland vista you couldn't imagine. To our left is the aquamarine sea, a distant sloop tacking on the sun-dappled horizon, a pair of peregrines playing on the salty Seven Sisters up-draught ahead. To our right, an earthy reflection of the ocean itself, are the undulating waves of this chalk landscape folding meringue-like all the way to the Weald. It is indeed stunningly beautiful.

The South Downs Way is either 100 or 103 miles long, depending on where you begin. It has two starting points, both on the outskirts of Eastbourne – one (coastal) is for walkers and one (inland) for riders. Through much of East and West Sussex, the route follows the Downs' tops, with regular dew ponds and waymarked detours to Weald villages. People have walked, ridden, driven, fought and traded along the South Downs for more than 5,000 years. The route consists of numerous prehistoric tracks and links from the coastal areas to the Wessex Downs, near Winchester.

In Hampshire, the route through the Meon Valley is less well signposted, but this is likely to change. The South Downs is in the process of being designated a national park, pending a public enquiry and a decision from the Secretary of State.

In the South Downs Justin takes the lead. We're heading down to the Seven Sisters Country Park, an AONB and SSSI, and along the River Cuckmere to Alfriston.

"Alfriston is just about the most picturesque Downland village, certainly in the east," he says. "There is a church known as The Cathedral of the Downs on the banks of the Cuckmere there, and the first ever National Trust property, the 12th-century Clergy House."

We head west along the cliff path, past the lighthouse at Birling Gap where the TV series The Lives and Loves of a She-Devil was filmed, and along the top of the Seven Sisters cliffs. From here we follow a waymarked path down to the wide, meandering Cuckmere valley, and then head north past Friston Forest and West Dean to Alfriston.

Above: Dew ponds pepper the South Downs.
Below: The Star Inn, where King Alfred burnt the cakes!

The village is home to the Star Inn, where King Alfred, arguably the first English monarch, was said to have burnt the cakes. Whether the Star Inn was indeed the site of Alfred's culinary disaster is a moot point. It is recorded that the king gave the area to one of his warlords, Aelfric, as a fief – a reward for valour in battle. He also visited West Dean when the English fleet was harboured there. Today, West Dean is the site of the Chalk Stones, 14 rocky white spherical forms by the landscape artist Andy Goldsworthy. I can't resist a pit-stop at the Star Inn and, as we enjoy some light refreshment (no burnt cakes to report today), my brother continues his commentary.

"We only have time to go as far as Chanctonbury Ring," he says, "which means you're not going to see the Hampshire bit of the trail. It's a beautiful section of the South Downs Way, but perhaps not as typically 'Downland' as the rest."

The Meon Valley is particularly attractive, with its beech hangers – or wooded hillsides – and the chalk-bottomed River Meon is a Mecca for anglers, as is the Itchen a few miles west.

Walk South

"It's only when you get up here that you can look down on everything, get a sense of perspective on what you've achieved and what you hope to achieve."

Walking Devils Dyke

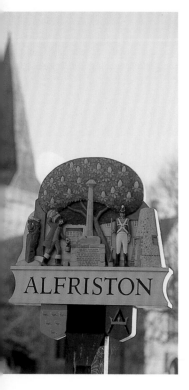

Two Neolithic sites, Beacon Hill and Old Winchester Hill, are both well worth a detour from the South Downs Way. And to get an idea of what Neolithic life on the Downs must have been like, the South Downs Way passes through Queen Elizabeth Park, which has a farmstead that practises agricultural and building techniques used in Neolithic times.

Suitably fortified at the Star Inn, we head west out of Alfriston up to Firle Beacon, with views over the opera house at Glyndebourne. Our path takes us across the Ouse, which flows through the town of Lewes, home to the Harveys brewery, which supplies many of the pubs around here. Just north is the village of Rodmell and the National Trust-owned Monks House, once home to Virginia and Leonard Woolf, and a frequent meeting place of the Bloomsbury Group.

Across the A27 and we head up to the Downs above Brighton, only a couple of miles south, and to Beacon Hill with its jaw-dropping views north.

"From here you can see all the way to your patch," says my brother. The Weald stretches out to the horizon, while the winking lights and brown-brick smudges of Sussex communities are adrift on an ocean of arable greens. And, in the distance, beneath the clouds, a ridge seemingly only a hand's grasp away – the North Downs Way.

We head west again and arrive at the Jack and Jill windmills above Clayton. "Jack, the black windmill, is privately owned," says Justin. "But Jill, the white windmill, has been restored by volunteers and occasionally produces organic stoneground wholemeal flour."

Across the A23 we head to Devil's Dyke, owned by The National Trust and comprising 200 acres of Downland scarp, deeply incised by a dry valley. A hotel sits on the site of an Iron Age fort. "Devil's Dyke is at the heart of a larger National Trust estate of nearly 700 hectares," says Justin.

Devil's Dyke extends west along the ridge of the Downs for about four miles, a route high above the villages of Fulking and Poynings, frequently buzzed by hang-gliders and paragliders.

We walk past the trig point and on to Fulking Hill. A tributary path to Fulking's Shepherd and Dog pub promises fine food and drink, as well as a garden carved out of a pleat in the Downs, brought alive by the music of a whispering stream.

"We'll pop in on the way back, says Justin, "but we have to get up to the radio masts and the youth hostel on Truleigh Hill, and then across the A283, for a real treat at the end of our walk."

Chanctonbury Ring is indeed a treat, a circular tree-clad mound visible for miles. It sits proudly on the northern edge of the South Downs overlooking the village of Washington, 783ft above sea level. It was an Iron Age fort, later occupied by the Romans. But it was the planting of beech trees by the 18th-century landowner Charles Goring that really gave this place some character.

Many of the trees blew down in the great storm of 1987 and some saplings have been planted since – it will be a while before Chanctonbury is back to its former glory.

This evening the sun is at large, bringing the Downs alive, but sending shadows of clouds across the Weald like great airships of darkness. At night the ring must have a foreboding feel. "The place does have some sinister connections," says Justin. "Witchcraft, fairies, UFOs, that sort of thing." But it also has an elemental application. An old Sussex saying goes that 'When Old Mother Goring's got her cap on, we shall soon have wet', meaning that when the ring is covered by cloud, expect rain.

We both look up. A cloud does seem to be brushing the tree tops. "Now tell me again about The Shepherd and Dog," I say.

The South Downs Way

Truleigh Hill, complete with radio masts

The trig point at the of Fulking Hill

Box Hill – home to more than two thirds of Britain's butterfly species.

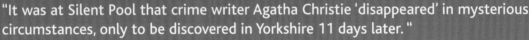

"It was at Silent Pool that crime writer Agatha Christie 'disappeared' in mysterious circumstances, only to be discovered in Yorkshire 11 days later. "

The North Downs are in some way the antithesis of their cousins in the south. Whereas the South Downs are bold and brash, and flaunt their opulent flanks of naked greens and whites, the North Downs are more reserved and prefer to hide beneath sandy woodlands and forests, behind sleepy villages, under arable crops or the hooves of grazing animals.

For some reason, the North Downs seem to lack the confidence of the ridge to the south. But appearances can be deceptive. It's true, the North Downs don't quite make the same audacious landscape statement as the South Downs. Yes, they are tied down and enmeshed with fences and hedges, criss-crossing roads and commuter-belt communities. And yes, while the South Downs enjoy potential national park status, the North Downs are perpetually threatened by airport expansions, European rail links and ever-growing motorway intersections and bypasses.

But for me, like a good book, it is the wealth of stories and anecdotes that the North Downs have to offer that make them worth the perusal. This understated, undulating ridge offers a secret escape for all those individuals living in the south of England. They are a veil through which many thousands of people have passed, and continue to pass, in order to step into a corridor of serenity, heritage and culture. They are, in fact, a walking history lesson – from St Swithun, to Geoffrey Chaucer and Jane Austen.

"But you can't see the sea!" snorts my brother, Justin, as I argue my case for the North en route to the Norman church perched atop St Martha's Hill in Surrey, a beautifully leafy lump to the east of Guildford, resplendent today in winter browns, reds and golds.

"Well, no, not here, admittedly," I say. "But the North Downs Way runs all the way to the White Cliffs of Dover and there's plenty of sea to be seen out there."

The North Downs Way runs for 141 miles from Farnham, in Surrey, through Canterbury to Dover, Kent. It is a route that follows ancient trackways along sand and chalk ridges, and wooded downland, through two Areas of Outstanding Natural Beauty, grazing the southern edge of greater London and ending at the celebrated cliffs over which Vera Lynn's bluebirds famously fly.

There are excellent transport links along the length of it – you can be on the North Downs Way within 20 minutes of leaving Victoria Station in the heart of London – and the route has a wealth of treats for the day walker (it can be easily divided into 13 sections, according to the official guidebook).

Right: The Downs link is well sign-posted
Below: The 11th-century Norman church of St Martha's

A family tree?

For most of its length, the North Downs Way runs parallel to the ancient trail known as the Pilgrim's Way, between Winchester and Canterbury. It was used by pilgrims on their way to pray at the shrine of St Thomas à Becket, who was murdered in 1170 at Canterbury Cathedral. The entire footpath was immortalised by Chaucer in his Canterbury Tales. Prior to this, pilgrims would have walked the other (east-west) way to pray for St Swithun, who was buried at Winchester.

Today we are telling The Brothers' Tale and, from Farnham, Justin and I soon leave the urban bustle and find ourselves relaxing into the soft, sandy trackways and mossy wooded paths that make up the early part of the Way. At Puttenham we stop off at the warm and walker-friendly pub, The Good Intent, for sustenance, before heading on to St Martha's Hill on Albury Down, east of Guildford.

"For me, St Martha's always feels like the start of the North Downs Way proper," I say to Justin. "It's only when you get up here that you can look down on everything, get a sense of perspective on what you've achieved and what you hope to achieve." We admire the view from St Martha's church, a charming 11th-century Norman edifice perched on the summit of the hill.

Walk North

Walking Devils Dyke

"At night the ring must have a foreboding feel. The place does have some sinister connections – witchcraft, fairies, UFOs, that sort of thing."

Below: Silent Pool, scene of an Agatha Christie mystery

Winter bracken carpets the wooded hillside, lending the North Downs area an intense copper brilliance. A kestrel hovers above some unfortunate prey in a field, in the valley below. In the distance, the rolling hills of the South Downs are just visible. "And, of course, this is the point where the South Downs Way and the North Downs Way are most connected," I say to Justin.

The Downs Link path runs from here all the way to Steyning, close to Chanctonbury Ring, and bridges the gap between the North Downs Way in Surrey and the South Downs Way in West Sussex. Much of this 30-mile route follows the track of a disused railway and can get very muddy, especially in winter.

We head down to Newlands Corner in the Tillingbourne Valley and then to Chantry Wood, the beginnings of a chalk path underfoot. From here, we make a small deviation south to Silent Pool, where the crime writer Agatha Christie 'disappeared' in mysterious circumstances, only to be discovered in Yorkshire 11 days later after one of the biggest man-hunts in history.

Today the pool is indeed silent – it would, perhaps, be a little more so were it not for the fact that the A25 runs past it a few hundred metres away. But what is more striking is the incredible clarity of the spring water. We stop for a spot of al fresco lunch and are treated to the electric-blue streak of a kingfisher on the wing.

At Box Hill, carved arrows indicate distant South Downs beauty spots

The North Downs, with its many ancient wooded areas and thickets, support a diverse range of animal life. As well as the occasional kingfisher, you might spot blue, great, coal, marsh and long-tailed tits, treecreepers, nuthatches and goldcrests. Butterflies form a special feature of the Downs during the spring and summer months and more than two thirds of Britain's butterfly species have been recorded at Box Hill, just outside Dorking.

Churchill, General Wolfe, Lewis Carroll, Charles Darwin and Charles Dickens all lived in, and were inspired by, the area. And the Battle of Britain was fought from Biggin Hill and over the Dover cliffs, making the North Downs themselves both literally and figuratively a runway to the heart of Britain. Finally, the route also takes in three cathedrals, three palaces and eight castles, including Leeds Castle, a fairytale moated stronghold once part of the dowry of English queens.

The sun is dipping now and it's time for a cup of tea. I'm not sure if I've sold the North Downs Way to my brother, but I have had a lot of fun trying.

Right: Denbies vineyard – seven miles of walking for wine lovers

Left: Winter Bracken on the Downs
Below: Neolithic Coldrum Stones in the Medway Valley

The largest vineyard in the UK, Denbies, lies below and ahead of us as we return to our path and head up the chalk scarp of Netley Heath and Oaken Grover, with their dense woods and herb-rich grasslands. The vineyard boasts seven miles of its own paths for the wine-loving walker, not to mention B&B for those who have indulged themselves perhaps a little too much.

From the vineyard, Justin and I cross the A24 and make the tough climb to the top of National Trust-owned Box Hill, so named because of the many box plants indigenous to its flanks. The climb is worth it. At Box Hill's crown is a semi-circular viewing station, with arrows carved into the stone indicating the location of a number of South Downs beauty spots, including Devil's Dyke and Chanctonbury Ring.

"Let's stop for a coffee," I say to my brother. "It is around here that Jane Austen's eponymous heroine is thought to have come for her picnic in the novel *Emma*." And, now it strikes me that it is the history and heritage that make the North Downs so special. At Otford, in Kent, the North Downs Way passes the UK's only listed pond, and in the Medway Valley the Way takes in the Neolithic Coldrum Stones, said to be linked by a tunnel to the church at nearby Trottiscliffe (pronounced 'Trosley').

Before you go...

No tender-hearted garden crowns,
No bosomed woods adorn,
Our blunt, bow-headed, whale-backed Downs
But gnarled and writhern thorn   *Rudyard Kipling*

More information

South Downs Way
Bill Jenman,
tel 02393 597618.

Sussex Downs
Conservation Board –
info on the downs,
including chalk stones,
tel 01903 741235,
www.vic.org.uk

North Downs Way
Tony Gowers,
tel 01622 221525.

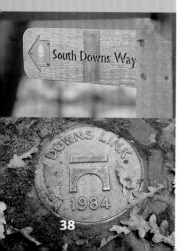

Food & Drink

Star Inn, Alfriston, East Sussex. Offers accommodation, good food and some fine local ales. The half-timbered pub dates from 1345 and is considered one of the oldest hostelries in the country. It is said to be built on the site where Alfred burnt the cakes. Tel 0870 400 8102.

The Good Intent, Puttenham, Surrey. A walker-friendly pub slap bang on the North Downs Way. The Good Intent offers plenty of home-made traditional English pub food, plus a generous roast on Sundays. Real ales on offer include Hogs Back Tea, Theakston's Old Peculiar and Ringwood 49er. Tel 01483 810387.

The Shepherd and Dog, Fulking, West Sussex. An 18th-century pub, with a footpath from the South Downs Way leading straight into its back garden. Excellent traditional English pub food, home-made pies and casseroles, plus fresh fish from the coast. A range of Badger ales and one of only four UK pubs to stock the noted Sussex beer Fursty Ferret. Tel 01273 857845.

Denbies Vineyard, Dorking, Surrey. The largest vineyard in the UK offers tours, accommodation, meals and wine tasting. Denbies has seven miles of footpaths to explore, two restaurants and a six-room B&B facility. In March the vineyard starts producing the previous year's rosé, so don't miss out. Tel 01306 876616.

Illustration: Steve Hall.

Maps

North Downs

Ordnance Survey Landrangers 177, 178, 179, 186, 187, 188 and 189.

Ordnance Survey Explorers 137, 138, 145, 146, 147, 148, 149 and 150.

Harvey Maps, North Downs Way West (Farnham to Medway).

Harvey Maps, North Downs Way East (Dover to Medway).

South Downs

Ordnance Survey Landrangers 185, 197, 198 and 199. Ordnance Survey Explorers 119, 120, 121, 122, 123 and 132.

Harvey Maps, South Downs Way.

There are also many excellent free guides and brochures about the North and South Downs, available from most tourist information centres throughout the area.

Francis Lord.

Chalk Stones walks

Landscape artist Andy Goldsworthy has sculpted 14 chalk stone spheres and placed them on a trail near West Dean, West Sussex. The stones will disintegrate over time, and their decay will be photographed and recorded in a book.
The Chalk Stones Trail is freely accessible to all, or you can join a guided walk of the area with experts, led by Footprints of Sussex. For more information, or to book your place, send a SAE to Footprints of Sussex, Pear Tree Cottage, Jarvis Lane, Steyning, West Sussex BN44 3GL.
The trail is easily accessible by public transport from either Chichester or Midhurst, with bus service 60 stopping at either end (Cocking Hill and West Dean).
For bus and train enquiries call Traveline on 0870 608 2608.

Peak 'n' mix

Eight fabulous routes, split into four delicious weekends.
With so much choice, asks Perry Cleveland-Peck, which
combination will you try first?

Pictures: **Tom Bailey**

From the bleak moors of Kinder Scout to the
gentle chalk streams of Grindleford, the scarred
landscape of industrial Eldon Hill to the elegant
lines of Chatsworth, the Peak District offers a wealth
of delights for every walker – little wonder that,
after Mount Fuji in Japan, the Peak is the most
visited national park in the world.

This extraordinary scenery persuades many of us
to pack our bags for holidays and short breaks, so we
can make the most of the seemingly endless miles of
inviting paths. But how can you find the best place to
stay? Which trails will make your next visit
unforgettable? And what can you do if the weather
turns sour?

To help you decide, here are four themed walking
weekends for you to pick and choose from...or mix
and match. All you have to do is relax, and prepare
for your best weekend in the Peak District...ever.

Monsal Trail

Where the 4.25pm from St Pancras once chuffed, you can today savour tranquillity. Opposite: Derwent Reservoir provided good target practice for the Dambusters.

"There are owls, merlins, and the bombers of 617 Squadron."

The Route

Distance: *13.8km/8 1/2 miles*

Route: *This walk is organised by the Peak District National Park, and booking is essential. Call 01298 871869.*

"You enterprised a railroad through the valley – you blasted its rocks away, heaped thousands of tons of shale into its lovely stream. The valley is gone and the Gods with it, and now every fool in Buxton can be at Bakewell in half an hour and every fool in Bakewell at Buxton; which you may think a lucrative process of exchange – you Fools everywhere."

The Victorian poet, Pancras. Speckled wood butterflies flit between common-spotted orchids, saxifrage and tufted vetch, while tumbling wild roses dance across views of the River Wye.

The natural history in this area is inspiring – a field across the Wye from Cressbrook is known as Bellamy's Bank, after an undergraduate David Bellamy came here on field trips and discovered his passion for botany. But, just as I become overwhelmed by the buzz and colour, a branch swings aside, revealing a vast steel doors.

"You're not afraid of the dark are you?" asks Clive Smith, one of the national park's 160 part-time rangers, who is accompanying me. I shake my head, perhaps a little too quickly. I mean, how dark can it be?

Perhaps it is just the sharp drop in temperature, but as the doors close with a boom straight out of a horror film, a chill runs through me. For a moment we're hushed. Only the drip-drip of water breaks the silence. The air is laced with soot and sulphur, and there's no chance my eyes can adjust to this terrible darkness. A torch beam arcs through the gloom, revealing fang-like stalactites hanging from the ceiling.

Refuges for the railway workers are set into the wall at regular intervals. One of them, in Lytton Tunnel, is much deeper than the others – remnants of a mined lead seam, perhaps, or a troll's lair?

Derwent Reservoir

Derwent is celebrated for its birds of prey. There are the goshawks and peregrine falcons. There are the owls, buzzards and merlins. And, of course, there are the Lancaster bombers of 617 Squadron, which bounced bombs into the dams of the Ruhr valley during the Second World War, using the Derwent and nearby Howden reservoirs for practise runs. You may have seen a film about it...

So, what with all this history – be it natural, chronological or celluloid – Derwent makes for fine walking. But who to guide me? A friend of a friend has put me in touch with a shadowy organisation known only as the Thursday Group – not a clandestine resistance movement still fighting to save the free world, but an offshoot of the Knutsford Ornithological Society, which goes walking on Thursdays.

John Somerville is my Agent X, and we have arranged to rendezvous below the imposing towers of Derwent Dam.

"The group has been walking on Thursdays for seven years now," he says. "We're all keen birdwatchers, but the aim of this group is to walk, and to take in as much as possible. We have a botanist, an archaeologist and a moth expert. Between us we cover quite a lot."

Which is just fine, because Derwent Reservoir offers a lot. The valley was flooded about a century ago, creating the Howden, Derwent and Ladybower reservoirs. These are sheer-sided, deep bodies of water, which echo to the calls of resident mallard ducks and sandpipers. The forests on the sides of the reservoirs are made up of natural oak and conifer plantations and the clay path we're walking occasionally twists through these to the water's edge. Above the trees, heathery moorland disappears to the skyline, "A good place to look for goshawks," says John, who is scanning the horizon through binoculars. "There are seven pairs here now. The first moved in about 15 years ago."

But if the goshawks have claimed the skies, sheep own the shoreline. We are all delightfully delayed while a lamb chooses our path as the place to have a good feed from mum. "This is where Birchinlee village used to be," says John. "Or Tin Town, as it was called. It was built to house workers during the construction of the dams."

And then my Agent X lets his cover slip. He reveals that, the last time he was here, he spied two of the ultimate killer flying machines. "Lancaster bombers, stealth fighters?" I ask, my heart thumping. No, a pair of peregrine falcons displaying in the air.

The Route

Distance: *15.3km/9 1/2 miles*

Route: *This is a circular walk around the Howden and Derwent Reservoirs. Start at King's Tree car park on the west side of Derwent Dam. Head south to Derwent Dam. Cross the reservoir beneath Derwent Dam, then walk north along a footpath to Slippery Stones, before heading south back to the start at Kings Tree.*

Kinder Scout

If there's one place in the Peak District every walker should visit, it's Kinder Scout. It was here that, in 1932, 400 people came to protest against the lack of public access in the country. As one old campaigner put it, "It seemed obscene that someone could treat great tracts of moor like they were private gardens."

The mass protest march started in Hayfield, but, in the interests of diversity (read masochism), I decided to approach Kinder Scout from Edale. It's a steep climb up Grindsbrook Clough, and I'm already feeling a little weary after the car journey here, although last night's trip to the pub may be a contributory factor. But my theory is that a walk across this untamed chunk of the Peak District will push plenty of much-needed fresh air into my lungs, and get my weekend off to an invigorating start.

I strike out a steady pace, zipping over a log bridge in the wooded Grindsbrook ravine, on to flagstones and the well-trodden mud path of Grindsbrook Clough itself. I have food and water to keep me going, plus a map and compass, and waterproofs and extra fleeces. I'm really starting to feel like some Grizzly Adams-type character – just me and the untamed hills. Then a small dog and a runner in shorts and T-shirt come bounding past, and the spring goes out of my step a little.

The climb is steady for a mile or two, the muddy path along the stream's edge turning to loose rocks and boulders as I gain height. The late afternoon has brought a freshening breeze, which cools me rapidly when I stop for a breather. Towards the final half-mile the gradient becomes steeper, and I'm forced to scramble over gritstone outcrops to reach the peaty top at Fox Holes.

But what a top it proves to be. At about 2,000ft above sea level, you can see the Win Hills and all the way to Lincolnshire. The early evening sunshine lights up the moors, giving this inhospitable and desolate landscape an incredible blue-grey intensity and a lonesome beauty. I soak up the atmosphere – and some water from my flask. Kinder Scout is not a place for the inexperienced walker – the mountain rescue teams are called out with depressing regularity – but the paths around its edges are navigable enough and offer spectacular views over the surrounding hills, valleys and reservoirs.

Go prepared and enjoy!

The Route

Distance: 10.5km/61/2 miles.
Route: *Walk north through Edale, following signs for Grindsbrook Clough. Head over the log bridge, through the plantation and up the clough to Edale Moor and Kinder Scout. At Fox Holes take a path south along the Kinder edge to Grindslow Knoll. Head south, then south west, then south east down the western edge of Broadlee-Bank Tor, picking up the Pennine Way at grid ref SK108855. Head east along the Pennine Way back to Edale.*

"People have been seeing things in the area for hundreds of years"

Haunted Valley

Prepare to be scared witless. This particular weekend is about to be rounded off with a spine-tingling walk at Longdendale, near Glossop. The valley is home to a freakishly high level of ghostly reports and unexplained phenomena, and considered by some as one of the most active 'windows' for sightings of UFOs and strange lights. There's even a website showing images from a camera trained on the valley 24 hours a day (www.hauntedvalley.com).

The area abounds with spooky legends and unexplained reports of such bizarre phenomena as ghostly aircraft, spectral Roman soldiers, moody mermaids, headless horsemen, devils and little green men. And reports continue to flood in all the time.

Country Walking beamed up Dr David Clarke, "People have been seeing things in the area for hundreds of years," says Dr Clarke. "Whether you call it Will O'The Wisp or UFOs, it is all unexplained folklore."

Dr Clarke's very own Haunted Valley Walk includes the Devil's Gate, a stream that another doctor is reported to have crossed 72 years ago in a bid to escape Satan himself. But, if our doctor's ghost walk has devils, it also features some more contemporary manifestations of unexplained happenings – the haunted crash sites of military aircraft.

"They all went down between 1945 and 1948," says Dr Clarke. "The pilots may have seen unexplained lights on the moors that confused them. You certainly experience eerie feelings at the site of the B29 Super Fortress, when the fog comes in. It is supposed to be haunted by the aircraft's captain, Captain Landon P Tanner, who crashed there in 1948. His engraved ring was found at the site only recently."

So does Dr Clarke really believe in UFOs and ghost lights? "I'm open-minded, but I think it has something to do with the geology of this area. Maybe the fault lines underground create stresses and strains in the rock that create strange energies..." It's all very X-Files.

Top: Kinder Scout – an invigorating start to any weekend
Opposite: Paths in Longdendale

The Route

Distance: *8.5km/5 1/4 miles*
Route: *This walk is partly over rough moorland, so a map and compass are essential. Start from the lay-by on the A57 at the summit of Snake Pass, where it meets the Pennine Way. Follow the Pennine Way north for 2km to Hern Clough. Come off the Pennine Way and head west over rough ground to the trig point on Higher Stones Shelf. The remains of a B29 Super Fortress are just north east of the trig point (grid ref SK091949). West of the B29, on James Thorn, are the remains of a Canadian Lancaster bomber (grid ref SK077948). From James Thorn, head down Ashton Clough. The remains of a US C47 Sky Train are scattered in the clough (grid ref SK082946). Drop to the valley floor and Devil's Gate Path (look out for men with horns and cloven feet) and head west to Glossop, enjoying the Longdendale panorama, some possible unexplained light phenomena and views over Glossop, Bleaklow and Woodhead.*

Mushroom Bounty

September is such a delightfully organic month. "Seasons of mists and mellow fruitfulness", as Keats put it. And one especially delightful manifestation of this "mellow fruitfulness" is the proliferation of fungi and toadstools, which squirm and seep and ooze from their hiding places at this time of year. September is ripe for a fungus foray.

"There's something magical about fungi," enthuses Rick Jillings, a ranger with the Derbyshire County Council Countryside Service. "People don't really understand them. There's a certain excitement about going out to hunt for something that could be poisonous or hallucinogenic…or could even kill you."

Rick is just one of the rangers who run guided fungi forays in the Black Rocks area of Derbyshire. Black Rocks, just off the High Peak Trail, has been a tourist destination for centuries; chiselled graffiti on the rocks go back hundreds of years. The area was, at one time, mined for lead and, even if you fail to find any mushrooms, keep an eye open for the lead-tolerant adder's-tongue fern and alpine pennycross, which have made the scree from the mines at Black Rocks their home.

But head into the forest behind Black Rocks and you should have no problems finding fungi. Unlike most of the Peak, which has an acidic and fungally less friendly limestone bedrock, Black Rocks and nearby Cromford Moor are based on gritstone, which is more alkaline and, therefore, suitable for mushrooms.

"This area is owned by the Forestry Commission," says Rick, as we step into the pine plantation near Fiveways. "This means there's public access and you can nip off the footpaths and into the undergrowth."

At the crossroads, Rick pulls up sharply, and sniffs. A smile plays across his face. Which is odd, because the aroma here is not exactly pleasant – rotten flesh springs to mind.

Encouraged by Rick, I get on hands and knees and bury myself under the damp bracken, expecting the worst. Then all is revealed. Stinkhorns! Fleshy, white protuberances with chocolate-brown caps, bursting out of grotesque egg-like mucus sacks.

So that's why these peculiarly seasonal, strangely beautiful species are thought of as neither plant, nor animal. These alien beings are surely from another planet!

The Route

Distance: *13.7km/ 81/2 miles*
Route: *From Black Rocks parking and picnic area (grid ref SK302558) head east on the High Peak Trail to Oak Farm. Take a path south to Intake Lane. Head north west along a lane back to the High Peak Trail. Retrace your steps for 230m. Climb the path southwards to Cromford Moor. In just over 100m the path veers right and heads towards a plantation. Head through the plantation and across Fiveways (the forest floor around here – grid ref SK298556 – should prove particularly fruitful for foragers) to the trig point. Take in the views before following a path north north east through Barreledge Quarry, then north west to Black Rock. Head east for the car park.*

Three Rivers

The arch is symmetrical, 30ft high and 23ft wide. The high ceiling is supported by limestone columns that run deep into the interior. Standing in the entrance, all are humbled by this magnificent edifice. We speak in hushed tones.

No, I'm not in Derby Cathedral, but Thor's Cave in the Manifold Valley, the highlight of an eight-and-a-half mile walk along the banks of the Manifold, Dove and Hamps rivers. And if Thor's Cave is not a cathedral, visiting it is certainly a divine experience. Lucky old Thor.

The cave was, at one time, considered the consummate des res (roomy, ample ventilation). Human beings have probably been dwelling in it since Palaeolithic times, and certainly since the Iron Age and Roman periods. Now only birds, bats and us walkers get to enjoy the views of craggy limestone configurations, blown and beaten into the most breathtaking shapes, that rear up from the Manifold valley floor.

I'm here to walk the waters that carved out Thor's Cave. The Manifold and its gorge-like valley walls are marked by pronounced bends. Indeed it is these meanders (or 'many folds') that give the river its name. The ancient woodlands that cover the valley walls have been designated a Site of Special

Top: River Dove, home to watervoles and orchids.
Bottom: Views like this, from Thor's Cave, inspired the ancients, too
Opposite: This is the perfect time of year for spotting fungi of all shapes, sizes...and smells

Scientific Interest. Ash, oak and wych elm make for a welcoming shady canopy as I head south, to where the Manifold meets the River Hamps. Field maple, hazel, holly, elder and bird cherry claim the walls lower down, while green swathes of large heart-shaped leaves carpet the banks of the river. "They're butterburr, or as some people call it, wild rhubarb," reveals Steve Massey, my companion for the day and the trees and woodlands officer at Staffordshire Moorlands District Council.

At the Hamps, we head up to the limestone grasslands of the Wetton Hills. These untouched grasslands are a rare habitat, supporting a diversity of plants for walkers to feast their eyes upon. Eyebright, mountain pansy and saxifrage decorate the paths, and, consequently, attract a wealth of buzzing insects and winking butterflies.

From Wetton, we head down Hall Dale to the River Dove, home to watervoles and orchids. Walking through such inspiring scenery is enough to make anyone forget about lunch, but my rumbling tum soon jolts me back to reality. Time for a sarnie and a refreshing cuppa.

The Route

Distance: 13.7km/8½ miles
Route: *Turn right out of the Carr Lane car park at Wetton (grid ref SK109552). Go right again then left on to a farm track. Follow the concessionary path to Thor's Cave. Take the steps down to the Manifold. Head south to Beeston Tor, where the Manifold meets the Hamps. Take a path north to a cattlegrid. Head east along Larkstone Lane, then south east along the ridge of Castern Wood. Take a path (grid ref SK118536) north east to where it joins a new path. Head south east to Damgate Farm, then north east to the top of Hall Dale. Head down to Dove Dale. Follow the River Dove to Mill Dale, then take a footpath south west to Stanshope and head north west back to Wetton.*

Chatsworth

Much has changed since the birth of walking as a pastime. Back in 1932, when Benny Rothman and his friends first took to Kinder Scout, the then Duke of Devonshire was so aghast at their audacity that five of the ring leaders were locked up. Recently, the present Duke of Devonshire, whose family home is Chatsworth, apologised for his grandfather's actions, and walkers dot his grounds like hats at Ladies' Day.

There's no doubt about it, Chatsworth is an

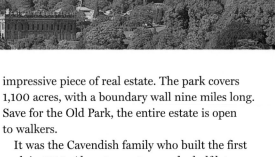

The Route

Distance: *11.3km/7 miles*
Route: *Park at Calton Lees car park. Take the footpath south through a farm and along the valley floor to Rowsley. Head north through the village and pick up a path heading north west along the valley side. Head north between Manners Wood and Lees Moor Wood to Calston House and, eventually, Edensor. From Edensor take a footpath west to Chatsworth. Follow the footpath south to Calton Lees. Alternatively, take one of the four walks through the grounds – Stand Wood Walk, Lovers' Walk, Water Walk or Edges Walk.*
Details are available from the Chatsworth Park guide.

impressive piece of real estate. The park covers 1,100 acres, with a boundary wall nine miles long. Save for the Old Park, the entire estate is open to walkers.

It was the Cavendish family who built the first park in 1549. Almost a century and a half later one William Cavendish was awarded a dukedom for his part in The Glorious Revolution of 1688, which saw James II booted out of Blighty by the Protestants, and he decided to rebuild the house totally at Chatsworth.

In the 1760s the fourth Duke of Devonshire commissioned 'Capability' Brown to improve the park. The result is what we see today. Oaks, yews, limes and Scots pine trees form belts around the edge of the park. The widened river creates a focal point and reflects the house. As picturesque as the landscape is, it's entirely man-made.

But today it's too hot to admire the baroque bricks and mortar. Stand Wood, behind the house, is much more inviting – and promises a few treasures. Amazingly, there wasn't a single tree in this area before the 18th century. Capability Brown started the planting, and it was continued by Sir Joseph Paxton, who started life at Chatsworth as an apprentice. He went on to design much of the landscape – not to mention Crystal Palace, which he based on Chatsworth's greenhouses.

While most people have hosepipes, Paxton wanted something a little more, well, elaborate.

The result was the enchanting – and intensely refreshing – aqueduct, built in 1840 to Paxton's designs as part of an ornate irrigation system for the park. The Swiss and Emperor Lakes, Ring Pond and Sowter Stone all supply water to the house and gardens, and, today, to a turbine that provides power to the house.

In late summer the stones of the aqueduct are covered by a variety of lush and verdant ferns but, according to the sixth Duke of Devonshire, "Nothing can be more beautiful than the icicles formed by the dripping from those arches."

Stone Circles

There are some places that are innately special. You just know it when you're there. You can just feel it. There's a spot about three miles south west of Bakewell which offers views over the surrounding limestone plateau so beguiling that, standing there, it is as if time has stopped. It is for this reason, some say, that a group of Neolithic craftsmen erected a monument here about 5,000 years ago, a stone circle hidden behind a circular bank. Five millennia later and people are still enjoying Arbor Low, even if they have little idea of its purpose.

"I always think of these places as a combination of a church, a marketplace and Glastonbury Festival," says Dr John Barnatt, senior survey archaeologist for the Peak District National Park. "A place for ceremonies, a place to exchange products, and a place to, well, get out of your head." On a late summer morning, under bruising skies, Arbor Low is certainly a place to let your imagination run riot. As I take a moment to enjoy views over the patchwork field landscape, lapwings singing on the soft breeze, I can't help but ponder how many others have been equally inspired by this heroic scenery. Arbor Low is considered the pre-eminent stone circle in the Peak District. It's the only upright stone circle, or henge, and is significantly larger than other circles. It originally had about 50 tall stones, with 10 more in the centre forming a central cove. "It would have taken a huge effort to build it, and there must have been an overwhelming desire to do so," says John. "The location is carefully orchestrated, which suggests the site was very important indeed."

Which makes it the perfect starting point for a walking history adventure. Based, loosely, on the Limestone Way, with a few tributary meanders for time travellers, this walk starts at Arbor Low and takes in a weird grotto, a second stone circle, an unusual natural rock formation, Hermit's Cave, Stanton Moor, a folly built for Earl Gray and some 19th-century royalist graffiti, before finishing at the Nine Ladies stone circle, nestled, as it is, in a bewitching grove of silver birch trees.

A few metres to the north west of Nine Ladies you'll find a single stone, the Piper Stone. Legend has it that the piper was playing his pipe for nine dancing ladies when they were all turned to stone. I prefer to think they all just decided to stay and admire the view for a while.

*Oppsite: The fern-covered aqueduct – an enchanting and cooling piece of irrigation
Left: Practise your climbing skills on Cork Stone, Satnton Moor*

The Route

Distance: *16km/10 miles*
Route: *From Arbor Low, head down a farm track. Turn right on Long Rake road. In 0.8km go left to Cales Farm. Proceed to One Ash Grange. Pick up the Limestone Way and head to where it meets the B5056 and Dudwood Lane – taking in Castle Ring at Harthill Moor Farm (grid ref SK222628), stone circle (grid ref SK225627), standing stone (grid ref SK225625), Robin Hood's Stride (grid ref SK224623) and Hermit's Cave (grid ref SK227624). Head north along the B5056 for 80m, then go right on to a footpath for Rocking Stone Farm. Continue to Birchover and take a footpath beneath Barton Hill Quarries to Birchover Road. Head up Birchover Road to Andle Stone. Retrace your steps for 80m. Take a footpath left (right as you come from Birchover) on to Stanton Moor. Go past Cork Stone and take a path left, heading north north west to Nine Ladies.*

Precious Stones

Walk from three limestone villages, jewels in the Cotswolds crown, for a brilliant weekend you will never forget.

When looking to buy a diamond, it is important to remember the 'Four Cs' rule. This maintains that while you may think big is best – and when it comes to diamonds, who wouldn't? – it is the quality that is all important, and this is ascertained by examining the carat, cut, clarity and colour of the stone.

In many respects, finding a location for a good walk is a similar exercise. All too often we walkers head for the big landscapes with the big skies, neglecting the more intimate places, often to be found on or close to our own doorsteps.

The Cotswolds is a case in point. Close to London, Wales, the south west and the midlands, this compact English region is prime walking territory, with footpaths cutting through it like the veins in a piece of malachite, rivers gin clear, and villages so picturesque even Hollywood couldn't dream them up – just look at the colour of the stone.

The Cotswolds is quality writ large. So forget the diamonds, and get yourself acquainted with the precious stones of the Cotswold villages instead. We have chosen three of them as 'base camps' for a perfect walking weekend. Try them out and we're sure you'll agree that the Cotswolds is every walker's best friend.

The Slaughters

Views to die for
in the place of pools

Crossing the River Eye by one of the many intimate stone bridges that are typical of Upper Slaughter

Whoever came up with the name 'Slaughters' for this beautiful part of the world was either mad or a genius. I mean, if you were looking for something to put people off visiting your village, calling it 'Slaughter' would certainly help. Perhaps that was just the point.

While researching this story, I had minds-eye images of abattoirs awash with blood, and steaming animal carcases hanging from chains. It almost stopped me visiting. So imagine my surprise when I arrived to find the most picturesque villages in England.

Upper and Lower Slaughter lie just north of Bourton-on-the-Water, and are linked by the River Eye. They exude charm and elegance and simple stone-hewn tranquillity.

The word slaughter, in this context, has nothing to do with blood and guts. Depending on where you look, it is either a derivation of the old English word 'slothre', or muddy place, which the villages may or may not have been at one time (but not today), or comes from the Saxon term for 'place of pools', which the Slaughters certainly are, or 'place of sloe trees', to which I can make no comment, not being a sloe tree expert in any shape or form. Whatever, I'm glad to be here.

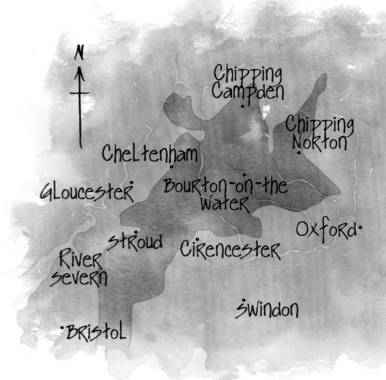

On a field track above the village of Naunton

"The Slaughters mark the start of a truly delightful route in the Windrush Valley that takes in real off-the-beaten-track villages such as Naunton and Temple Guiting..."

In spite of the name, the Slaughters are not as unspoilt as some might imagine. Tourists arrive by the coach load. But, cleverly, in my opinion, there isn't much actually to do in the villages, there being no pubs, clubs or restaurants to speak of. So, what with finding a parking space and whizzing around the 'attractions', such as they are, the tourists go again pretty quickly. Indeed, spend more than an hour here and you begin to feel like an old-timer.

However, for us walkers it's different. The Slaughters mark the start of a truly delightful route in the Windrush Valley that takes in real off-the-beaten-track villages such as Naunton and Temple Guiting, unspoilt by commercialism, tourism or the 21st century. Here, walkers can while away a happy day playing the 'would I live there' game and soaking up the glorious countryside.

Today, Country Walking's Katy, Nicola and I are on our best behaviour. Our editor, Jonathan, has joined us, and we are keen to demonstrate how hard-working and professional we all are, and how we are not the unprepared amateurs we suspect that he suspects he has for his team. So it is a real shame that, as the man with the map, I manage to get us lost twice (the first time I think I got away with it, talking about the lovely view that I wanted to share with my colleagues; but any fumbling

excuse about the second 'scenic route' was marred by the arrival of gentlemen on tractors who helpfully pointed out where I had gone wrong, in no uncertain terms).

It had been fine until Upper Slaughter. We had walked the banks of the shallow Eye, crossing the intimate footbridges and admiring the stone cottages and the somewhat incongruous brick-built watermill. But at Upper Slaughter we were forced to retrace our steps before heading off on the Wardens' Way, up through arable fields and then down a cool wooded section, close to the remote Cress Cottages. Across the road and into Eyford Park, where, distracted by some vocal cattle, we went far too far along the valley, missing Brockhill Farm and the footpath to Naunton.

Still, a short road-hike later and we are on the correct trail, on the hills above Naunton, the village winking in the trees below us.

I'm thinking that if I placate the editor with lunch at the pub there, and perhaps show him the 500-year-old dovecot for which the village is famous, and then treat him to a pint or two at the Hollow Bottom in Temple Guiting after our afternoon walk, I might just be around for the next edition of the magazine.

The Route

Tranquil villages in the Windrush Valley
Distance: *12.5km/7³/4 miles.*
Time: *5 hours.*
Terrain: *Field paths, woodland and village streets.*
Route: *From hotel (grid ref SP165225) follow river west out of the village (take path around back of watermill). Head north west to Upper Slaughter and pick up the path heading north to Cress Cottages. Pass cottages and take a left on to new road at Brockhill Farm. Pick up path (SP126243) south then west to Naunton. From Dovecot, head south, crossing road toward's Lodges Barn. Head east to Lower Harford and follow River Windrush to mill (SP148213). Pick up Macmillan Way north east to Lower Slaughter.*
Map: Ordnance Survey Explorer OL45, Landranger 163

Winchcombe

Haunted burial mounds, hooded figures and Castles

Perry on the path to Belas Knap, with views of Winchcombe and the Vale of Evesham beyond

The Route

Sudeley Castle and Belas Knap

Distance: *9km/5 1/2miles.*
Time: *3 hours.*
Terrain: *Grassy footpath, farm tracks.*
Route: *Head south from High Street (grid ref SP024282) on road to Sudeley Castle. Pick up Cotswold Way at castle gates and head to Humblebee Cottages. Head south west to road, then north along road for 180m for the path to Belas Knap (SP021254). Return to Humblebee and head south, then north east, to Newmeadow Farm. Pick up footpath east to Windrush Way. Head north to Sudeley.*
Map: *Ordnance Survey Explorer OL45, Landranger 163.*

No matter how much I look, the hooded figures elude me. Perhaps I'm not trying hard enough. Or maybe I just don't have the technique 'down', as the Americans say. This time, I scan the landscape through tightly squinted eyes, fingers crossed and with breath held. But the rolling, almost downland hills, musty post-harvested swathes, punctuated with lazily undulating green hedgerows and the occasional woody copse, appear perfectly normal. Nope, there are no strange hooded figures here today. Well, apart from our damp photographer Tom, who often takes on a haunted appearance when working with me.

I've been told, you see, that Belas Knap, the neolithic burial mound that goes back to before the Romans, and upon which I currently have the pleasure of standing, is home to some pretty unusual activity of the paranormal type.

One recent report has it that when a female walker reached the top of Belas Knap, she saw a group of hooded figures marching briskly across an adjacent field, though, strangely, never seeming to get closer. Concerned that she and her family were about to be disturbed, she climbed down to raise the alarm. But when nobody appeared, she returned to the top of the mound to find that the field was empty and "looked different". There were

fewer trees, the path had altered, and what had previously seemed to be a dip in the ground was now barely apparent. Spooky.

But today the hooded figures are keeping coy, and I have to content myself with kestrels on the wing, and the views over Winchcombe and the Vale of Evesham beyond, which take the word sweeping to a whole new level.

Winchcombe, the base camp for our Belas Knap walk, is itself no stranger to peculiar goings-on. Its appropriately named Cowl Lane is said to be haunted by hooded monks, though some believe these figures, like those at Belas Knap, are spectral representations of the Cucullati, a Pagan-Romano British cult that was based in nearby Cirencester. This theory was lent credence by the recent discovery of a carved stone depicting hooded Cucullati, which was found in a well at Lower Slaughter and is now in Cirencester's museum.

But I'm not here for a ghost walk. Winchcombe and its surrounding countryside has more than enough natural phenomena to offer the walker, without having to resort to any of the 'super' variety. Today, I'm walking a loop from Winchcombe that takes in both Belas Knap and Sudeley Castle, the resident country pile that was once home to Catherine Parr, the last of

Henry VIII's wives, as well as the tragic and beautiful Lady Jane Grey, queen of England for nine days. It's now owned by the young aristocrat Henry Dent-Brocklehurst who, with his model wife Lili Maltese, regularly appears on the pages of Hello! magazine. But there are many other walks and landmarks to be enjoyed from Winchcombe – the Cotswold Way, Cleeve Hill and the atmospheric remains of Hailes Abbey included.

Earlier, I had walked out of Winchcombe, following the Cotswold Way past Sudeley and through damp fields, past an enchantingly set and delightfully proportioned farmhouse for Humblebee Cottages and the brief diversion over the road and up the hill to Belas Knap. Now,

"One report has it that when a female walker reached the top of Belas Knap, she saw a group of hooded figures marching across an adjacent field."

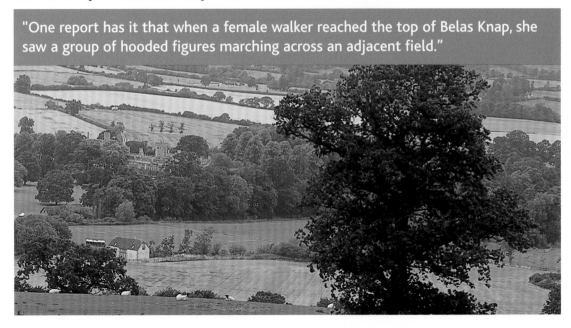

Left: Sudeley Castle, nestled in the folds of classic Cotswolds countryside

standing on the ridge above Winchcombe, with the burial mound behind me and Sudeley Castle nestled in the valley below, the sun illuminating occasional fields and woodlands like a spotlight following the lead actor on stage, I am seriously contemplating whether this is, in fact, the best view in the Cotswolds. It must be one of them. Surely.

But with the autumn skies a-brooding, it's time to head back to Humblebee for the Windrush Way, a mid-distance Cotswold village trail that will take me back to Sudeley or on to its junction with another Cotswold path, the Warden's Way, which,

like the Windrush Way, runs all the way from Winchcombe to Bourton-on-the-Water, but unlike the Windrush Way follows a more rural path, showing a more bucolic face of the Cotswolds.

I opt for the Sudeley route and descend to Beesmoor Brook, and then follow it north to the castle, crossing the brook about halfway up. But my walk isn't over yet. There are 14 acres of award-winning gardens to be explored at Sudeley, including an Elizabethan knot garden, and perhaps a well-earned cream tea to be devoured in the castle's baronial Banqueting Hall.

Bibury

The village for which chocolate boxes and picture postcards were invented

Above: Right: 'Catch your own' trout at the farm in Bilbury

Opposite: Bibury's Arlington Row – is there a more picturesque spot to check your map?

The Route

Pretty as a picture

Distance: *10km/6 1/4 miles.*
Time: *4 hours.*
Terrain: *Field tracks, some woodland and riverside paths.*
Route: *From Arlington Row (SP115066) pick up footpath north to road. Turn left and head uphill to pub. Pick up path south east. At junction, head south west. Take path (SP107063) south east to Coneygar Cottages and pick up path east to Coln St Aldwyns. Return via River Coln.*
Map: *Ordnance Survey Explorer OL45, Landranger 163*

At first I get excited about the trout. I have enough fishing friends, you see, to know that to catch a glimpse of these singularly shy and beautiful fish is a rare treat indeed, and one for which a river-roaming sportsman with rod and fly trains his eyes over many years. It's half the battle, apparently.

But here at Bibury, the trout are so plentiful and large, and the river so gin clear, that once I've spotted "another one!" and "look, another one!", and "good God, did you seen the size of that one!", the novelty begins to wear off. Indeed, after five minutes of river gazing I get the distinct impression that were I to take my boots and socks off for a little impromptu paddling, the trout would climb on to my shoulders and pose for photographs.

The river at Bibury is right next to one of the oldest trout farms in the country, and I guess that a couple or three of the up-to-10-million-a-year brown and rainbow-coloured blighters that are spawned here must have jumped the fence for a life of sandwich-munching leisure in the River Coln, which runs through this quintessentially Cotswold village.

Or two villages, in fact. Because Bibury is just one half of this Cotswolds treat, the other being Arlington and its eponymous Row just across the water to the west, which, between them, have over the years grown and merged and fused into one another, and now come under the single Bibury banner.

It is said that the British designer and figurehead of the Arts and Crafts movement, William Morris, once referred to Bibury as the most beautiful village in England. And when you cross the Coln by way of one of the many charming pedestrian bridges, and pass the marshy National Trust-owned bird sanctuary called Rack Isle (so named because it was here that the locally manufactured cloth was 'racked' after washing and dyeing) and step out on to Arlington Row, it is hard to disagree with the Victorian polymath. Arlington Row is surely why chocolate boxes and picture postcards were created.

But (somehow) I drag myself away from this idyllic collection of former weavers' cottages, and head north along the back of Rack Isle towards the trout farm and the old mill, now a craft museum and very fine tea shop, for a circular walk along the ridge above Bibury, to the adjacent village of Coln St Aldwyns, and then back again, bimbling the banks of the Coln itself.

My mother tells me that you can have too much of a good thing. Perhaps she is right. And while I don't believe it possible to overdose on Bibury, the sweeping naked fields that gradually replace the stone buildings of the village, and the blast of blustery autumn air that encourages me to pick up my pace, all seem like a refreshing deviation from the heady charms of the chocolate-coated community behind – like a light sorbet after a particularly rich supper. I press on with gusto.

I settle on the footpath that runs between Arlington Pike and Coneygar Cottages, buoyed by the cool breeze and bruising skies – I just love walking at this time of year, head down and into the wind, the smell of damp dogs hanging on the thickening air. Earlier I'd been told that the 12th-century church at nearby Quennington is dedicated to St Swithun and that, strangely, his name is linked with rain. And all of a sudden, as I cross the Akeman Street Roman road, this notion seems to add up and I stop to dig out my waterproofs.

But St Swithun's little offering doesn't matter. If anything, it enhances this start-of-season walk. And I have Quennington and its precipitous church to explore, and then the village of Coln St Aldwyns, with its charming old post office over three floors and ancient chestnut tree, and the river, of course, with its guileless trout, and where on Boxing Day the villagers hold their annual duck race.

Then there's the viking tombstone that is hidden in the wall of St Mary's at Bibury. And the Swan Hotel, and the walk tomorrow to Ablington. No, a little bit of rain doesn't matter at all.

"The British designer and figurehead of the Arts and Crafts movement, William Morris, referred to Bibury as the most beautiful village in England."

Before you go...

The Slaughters

Accommodation

Greenfingers, Lower Slaughter

Tastefully furnished ground-floor accommodation with fine views, set in a one-and-a-half-acre garden. Tel: 01451 821217

Washbourne Court Hotel

The only hotel in The Slaughters. Posh, but not unreasonably priced. It has 25 rooms and a restaurant.

Tel: 01451 822143 or visit www.washbournecourt.co.uk

King's Head Inn, Bledington

Les Routier's Central England Pub of the Year 2003 and County Dining Pub 2001, The King's Head is well worth a visit. Great food, well-prepared and using locally sourced produce wherever possible – the Aberdeen Angus beef comes straight from the neighbouring farm. Accommodation is over 12 rooms.

Tel: 01608 658365 or visit www.kingsheadinn.net

Watermill, Lower Slaughter

A 19th-century flour mill with huge waterwheel on the banks of the Eye. Now a museum.

Tel: 01451 820052.

Don't miss

The Dovecot, Naunton

Grade II-listed dovecot in Naunton that's being restored (grid ref SP118234). Retains its original interior and has a riverside setting for all to enjoy.

The Rollright Stones, Little Compton Collection of neolithic stone monuments (grid ref SP296309) – the King's Stone, a weathered and grotesque single standing stone; the Whispering Nights, a small collection of standing stones; and a magnificent stone circle, considered the third most important in the UK.

Visit www.rollrightstones.co.uk

Chastleton House, Chastleton

One of England's finest and most complete Jacobean houses, now owned by The National Trust. It was here in 1865 that the rules of modern croquet were codified.

Tel: 01608 674355 or visit www.nationaltrust.org.uk

Winchcombe

Accommodation

White Hart Inn, Winchcombe

A 16th-century coaching inn whose Swedish owners have brought a distinct Scandinavian feel – as well as steak and chips you can try a traditional Swedish smorgasbord. There are eight rooms, each decorated to a Swedish theme. The Carl Larsson room is influenced by the Swedish artist and designed in the style of his own home.

Tel: 01242 602359 or visit
www.the-white-hart-inn.com

Don't Miss

Sudeley Castle, Winchcombe

Tour the castle apartments or walk around the 14 acres of award-winning gardens of this historic residence. Or join Sudeley's 10km Stride For Life sponsored walk, on October 26th.

Tel: 01242 602308 or visit
www.sudeleycastle.co.uk

Bibury

Accommodation

Lavender Cottage, Bibury

The one large room available in this 400-year-old Grade II-listed building has views from three windows. Cereals and cooked breakfasts are provided, and local produce is used wherever possible. Vegetarians are also catered for. Luxurious, possibly the most economical B&B in Bibury

Tel: 01285 740205.

The Catherine Wheel, Bibury

A 15th-century pub featuring exposed original ship's timber beams, plus many prints and photographs of old Bibury. The Arlington Bar offers a fine choice of beers and wines.
There are four rooms to choose from.

Tel: 01285 740250.

Don't Miss

The Trout Farm, Bibury

One of the oldest trout farms in the country – it was founded in 1902 – and certainly the most attractive. Primarily a working farm, it has welcomed visitors since 1965.

Tel: 01285 740215.

Arlington Mill, Bibury

Arlington was one of the biggest mills in the area in the 19th century. Today, the mill is a museum displaying working machinery as well as pictures from its past. The mill also houses a tea room and gift shop.

Tel: 01285 740368.

Information

Visitor information centres

Hollis House,
The Square,
Stow-on-the-Wold

Tel: 01451 831082.

Victoria Street,
Bourton-on-the-Water

Tel: 01451 820211.

The Corn Hall,
Market Place,
Cirencester

Tel: 01285 654180.

Tourist information centre,
The Town Hall, High Street,
Winchcombe

Tel: 01242 602925.

Useful websites:

www.cotswold.gov.uk/tourism

www.visitcotswoldsand
severnvale.gov.uk

www.oxfordshirecotswolds.org

www.cotswolds-calling.com

www.cotswoldsinfo.com

Drystone walls, windswept moors, golden colours – it all adds up to typical Lancastrian scenery around Winter Hill.

Moors than meets the eye

Feast on the hotpot of paths that criss-cross Lancashire's West Pennine Moors.

Words: **Perry Cleveland-Peck** Pictures: **Andy Latham**

I'd been through it, of course. Many times. Mostly on my way to the Lake District. But had I known about this 'compact Cumbria' before, I'd have parked up right here. For Lancashire's West Pennine Moors, just a stone's throw south of the Lakes, has as much to satisfy a walker's appetite as the hotpot this county is famous for.

And satisfying appetites is what this particular walking adventure is all about, be they of a historical, natural, walking or gastronomic nature. Indeed, having explored the 90 square miles of delicious diversity that the West Pennines have to offer – a veritable hotpot of routes in itself – there's no doubt that you'll require a feast to match.

Lead Mines Clough

It is bucketing down as my old photographer friend Andy and I pull on our waterproofs, and set out for Lead Mines Clough. But, in a way, all this precipitation is oddly appropriate. You see, we are beginning this particular walking tour of the West Pennines with that most fundamental of raw materials in mind – water.

As with most places, water has played – and continues to play – a key role in the development of the people and landscape here. Yes, it's the basic ingredient of most drink and food, the Lancashire hotpot notwithstanding, but in Lead Mines Clough on Anglezarke Moor, on the western edge of the West Pennines, evidence of how man harnessed the water around him is manifest.

Right: Perry picked a peck of pitted Pike Stones...

Apart from a brief period in the 1780s, lead mining operations here were never entirely successful, and stopped altogether in 1837. And were it not for some excavation work completed in the area in the 1980s, lead mining on Anglezarke Moor may well have been forgotten entirely. Now, however, you can walk the length of charming Limestone Brook and be constantly reminded of how this intimate leafy clough, with its whispering birch trees and constant musical accompaniment of hissing cascades and gurgling, whisky-coloured rock pools, was once alive with the rhythmical clunks and clicks of heavy industrial machinery.

Andy and I leave the track and squelch over a bridge for a kissing gate and the path upstream. On our left is the first piece of our aquatic archaeology. The ignominiously named 'slime pit' played an important role in the mining of lead here. The shallow hollow in the earth is where particles of lead, brought down in water used for washing the ore, were retained. This lead-rich silt was then dug out and exploited, another raw material the earth offers up.

Across the stream is the small dark hole of the 'sough' – an area used for draining the workings. And a little further on are the remains of a waterwheel pit, which had the essential job of pumping water from the mine shaft.

For aqua-heads, there are some delightful waterfalls to be relished further up the brook, but all these ancient structures have put me in mind for some more history.

A footpath behind the wheel pit heads up through bracken to the moors above. A war

> "Walk the length of this intimate leafy clough, with its whispering birch trees and constant musical accompaniment of hissing cascades and gurgling, whisky-coloured rock pools."

memorial just off the path pays tribute to the crew of a Wellington bomber that crashed on the moors nearby in November 1943. Two benches thoughtfully placed offer a moment's peaceful reflection on this, not to mention moorland views across to Rivington Pike and Pigeon Tower, and Winter Hill with its own series of 1,000ft radio towers that dominate the skyline for miles around.

Up and over a ladder stile, and Andy and I are on to the moors proper, bleak in the drizzle but marked by occasional tufts of bright gorse and purple heather. We're walking alongside a recent plantation, not marked on my map, to an enclosed area that protects a chambered cairn – the oldest man-made structure around here.

There isn't much left of the Pike Stones now, just a few pieces of stone among lumpy windswept tussocks. But standing here, with views over the distant moors, you certainly appreciate that early Lancashire man was not entirely unaware of the concept of 'location'. A mile or so north east is Round Loaf, another neolithic burial chamber that looks for all the world like a steaming hotpot on the misty, otherwise featureless, Anglezarke Moor.

Beautiful Limestone Brook froths through Lead Mines Clough. Be sure to pack your camera.

West Pennine Moors

Blackburn

Accrington

M65

Darwen

A6177

Haslingden

M61

Great Hill

Musbury Heights

Tor Hill

Lead Mines Clough

Black Dog

N

Winter Hill

Lever Park

A675

Bolton

Kendal

Liverpool

The Route

Distance: *11.7km/71/4 miles*
Start: *Park at Anglezarke Reservoir car park (SD621161) or on the lay-by by Alance Bridge. Walk along western bank of Limestone Brook. Take path west to war memorial and follow plantation north to Pike Stones (SD638182). Head north east to Great Hill and pick up flagged path south to Spitlers Edge, before heading west back to car park.*

Great Hill

"The skies are blue – a colour I had almost forgotten since getting here."

Much of this job is spent chasing weather. I can spend days organising itineraries for features – meet A at X for an interview at 11am, then B at Y for a walk at 2pm – only for the forces above to take my plans and scatter them to the four winds. So a 'carpe diem' initiative is often called for. And so it was that, while Andy and I were dashing to reach a village near Blackburn before the shops closed for lunch, the clouds parted and the moors around Great Hill lit up like a recently renovated Van Gogh. "Park the car," I said. "The packed lunches can wait."

Andy had told me about Great Hill, the third highest peak in the West Pennines. From the top you can see west to the Irish Sea, north to the Lake

Right: White Coppice – the perfect setting for a cricket pitch.

The Route

Distance:
13km/8 miles
Start: *Park at car park (SD665191). Cross A675 and pick up path to Pimms and then Great Hill.
Head west to Drinkwaters and views of White Coppice. Head north to Brinscall, then east to Watson's Farm. Cross A675 and follow path south to car park.*

District, south east to Kinder Scout, east to nearby Darwen Tower on Darwen Hill and, further on, to Inglebrook in the Dales. Winter Hill, with its constant blinking aerials and towers – a contemporary reminder of this area's links with industry – frowns down at us from just a few miles to the south.

Today the path to Great Hill is wet. My boots sink to the laces with every footstep. But I'm feeling relatively snug, fleeced and water-proofed as I am, and we both make our way to the top of Great Hill, invigorated by the pleasure of this impromptu adventure. The skies above are blue – a colour I had almost forgotten since getting here – and the grassy moors have taken on their characteristically carrot-coloured hue. We climb happy. The path is steep, but eases out towards the top beside some ruined farm buildings.

But how the tables can turn. No sooner do we make the wind shelter (four stone walls built like a cross, aligned with the compass points) at the top of Great Hill, than a vast curtain of blackness sweeps in from the Irish Sea. Watching its progress, and how it seems to swallow up everything in its path, is compelling; the certain knowledge that we are about to be devoured, the anticipation of having to sit through it.

The rains hits, then the sleet, then the hail and, finally, some snow. But it is the wind that really cuts through – what I would do for a hot cup of tea!

The weather eases and we decide to investigate the slabbed path to Winter Hill. I am unsure of what to make of this path. Is it an abomination to have these man-made slabs cut through wide open moorland, or a sensible way of maintaining the path's width in all this wet? The slabs, Andy tells me, have come from a local, now-defunct, textile factory. I ponder the irony that they were originally cut from quarries on the moors around here, to create this works site, only to be returned to the moors with the factory's demise. I decide in the end that their presence is a good thing – they certainly make the going easier in the damp.

We stop for a while and admire the Round Loaf burial chamber from a new perspective (the last time I saw Round Loaf was from Pike Stones), before heading back to Great Hill and the path west to White Coppice. This chocolate box location, an award-winning hamlet, tucked from the outside world in a virtual cul-de-sac, was, surprisingly, a hive of industrial activity during the 19th century. It once boasted a handful of factories and mills, as well as many more homes to house the workers. Now, a string of small dams are the only testimony

to the industrial heritage.

The cricket pitch at White Coppice must surely be the most delightfully set ground in the country – and, if you're lucky, a good place for refreshments. But, with more rain, and the chance of an increasingly sticky wicket, Andy and I head back to Great Hill along the path we used earlier, past a ruined farmhouse at Pimms and on to the car.

Now, about those packed lunches...

Lever Park

The follies of Lever Park – too good to mist

> "Drystone walls meander ahead, offering tantalising half-glimpses of the rolling landscape to come."

The Route

Distance: 7.2km/41/2 miles

Start: *From Great House Barn visitor centre (SD629139). Head south along Lower Rivington Reservoir's eastern bank to The Castle. Head east to Higher Knoll and up to Rivington Pike. Head north west to Pigeon Tower (SD639144) and descend back to the car park through Lever Park.*

I try to avoid landscaped landscapes, so to speak. Don't get me wrong, I love gardens and all things green-fingered, but when I go for a walk I usually require something a little less refined – but, hey, that's probably just me!

But on Andy's suggestion, I decide to bend this self-imposed rule and explore the lost gardens of Lever Park at Rivington, on the south-western edge of the West Pennine Moors.

Rivington is the old estate of the de Rivingtons, which after several changes in ownership was bought in 1900 by one William Hesketh Lever, of Sunlight Soap fame. In 1902 the ennobled Lord Leverhulme donated this park to the people of Bolton. He had terraced grounds built here, with Japanese tea gardens and a handful of follies, including Pigeon Tower, which dates from 1910 and has to be the most elaborate dovecote in Lancashire. Rumour has it that this was where Lady Leverhulme came for a little light needlework.

After Lord Leverhulme's death in 1925, the gardens and follies were left to rack and ruin, but in the 1970s the site was partially restored. The result is a beguiling area of overgrown pathways, leafy oak woods, hidden steps and half-lost stone buildings that, in today's mist, seem like something from the Brothers Grimm. You can obtain a selection of guides from the information centre at Rivington Park, or you can do it my way – just get out there and explore. It's a lot more fun...for children of all ages!

Tor Hill

Tor Hill has to be the shapeliest mound in the West Pennines. It lies serenely and comfortably above the village of Helmshore, famed for its links with the textile industry and a museum celebrating this history. With its fringe of rocky crags and wispy clouds, it looks for all the world like some crusty loaf straight from the oven.

The climb to the summit is leisurely enough. Footpaths and farm tracks from Helmshore skirt its flanks and a concessionary path takes you to the top. Today the ground is wet, and I am thankful for the grip the rough Lancashire stones underfoot afford me at the start of this climb. Drystone walls meander ahead, offering tantalising half-glimpses of the rolling landscape to come. The rain-sodden moss on the wall tops winks and glistens in the sunlight, like emeralds set in stone. A handful of unamused moorland sheep, the likes of which constitute the staple ingredient of the food around here, chew nonchalantly as we pass by.

The footpath runs right through the back garden of what must be one of the most enchantingly set cottages in the whole of the West Pennines. It is perched at the base of Tor Hill's northern flank, and has sweeping views over Helmshore and the reservoirs of Musbury Heights to the north, with their leftovers of this area's industrial past.

Much of my time in the West Pennines has been spent in frustrating low visibility, like being blindfolded in an art gallery. Today, however, the elements have conspired to take pity on me, and the view from the top of Tor Hill is the stuff of all walkers' dreams. Sunlight on the moorland below sets the winter grasses ablaze with an orange luminescence, the shadows of clouds above occasionally bruising the fells. A pair of shire horses play with a pony below. In the distance, a peculiar finger-like rock structure on Musbury Heights beckons. For me, moments such as these are what walking is all about.

Above: Tor Hill – a walk for the upper crust?

The Route

Distance: *8.4km/51/4 miles*
Start: *Park in Helmshore. Pick up footpath (SD779213) running west to Tor Hill. Head around Tor Hill, west then north to Musbury Heights. Head south east back to Helmshore.*

Below: A reservoir outlet valve – evidence of the area's industrial heritage

Musbury Heights

The 'finger-like formation' seen from Tor Hill turns out to be the remains of a chimney

If Tor Hill was warm and inviting earlier today, Musbury Heights, just a few miles north, is its antithesis, like climbing to the gates of Hades.

Darkening skies and driving rain herald our hunched, head-down ascent. Chattering crows screech at our intrusion, the corpse of a long-dead moorland ewe stares out at us as we pass it on our way up.

Don't get me wrong, Musbury Heights is an exciting place to explore, invigorating and more than enough to get a walker's pulse racing. Andy and I had debated attempting the Heights from Tor Hill, but with the failing light and ominously heavy clouds, we decided to get to the top quickly. Having parked above Ogden and Calf Hey reservoirs, we crossed the Calf Hey dam for the path that runs east-west along the northern base of Musbury Heights, part of the 45-mile Rossendale Way that criss-crosses the West Pennines.

A little way up and we come to a brook that cleaves the hillside and our path, the inevitable torrent from a cascading crag on the rain-sodden hillside to our right. Today, the rock and mud path to the top also resembles something of a mountain stream, and I'm glad to be wearing my gaiters (though I wish I'd had the foresight to pack some overtrousers). On our left, just south of our path, are the remains of a once-thriving sheep farm, sombre and forbidding in the half-light.

The Heights themselves were at one time the site of some vast hilltop quarry. The strange finger-like rock formation I saw from Tor Hill turns out to be a crumbling works chimney. The shells of industrial buildings and work site outhouses litter this strangely undulating landscape. Stony door frames and collapsed lintels lie like ragged skeletons on a windblown battlefield.

Today, in the gloom and unrepentant drizzle, this place is indeed reminiscent of some long-forgotten theatre of war. The Heights are scarred by quarrying, with bubbling man-made hillocks of slag towering over deeply cut cart tracks to the rock face. The sheer stone elevations are so thick and well packed in places, it is impossible to tell whether these seemingly perfect thick, drystone constructions are a product of Mother Nature or a group of Lancashire masons. The entire place has a godless air, a place where troglodytes fought the ogres in a time before man. I love it.

As I stand and admire the chimney, reflected as it is in a small pool on the hillside, it occurs to me that these bruised and scarred places have a special resonance all of their own, that man can be ingenious in harnessing the materials around him but that nature always has the last laugh. And that ugliness can have a beauty all of its own.

"Dwarfed by aerial masts, this must be the only trig point with an inferiority complex."

Winter Hill

The leftovers of man's work on the moors are being slowly swallowed by Mother Nature

Winter Hill, with its trademark towers and aerials, is the highest peak in the West Pennines, at 1,496ft. A summit trig point, so often the lone, proud sentinel of many a mound, is simply dwarfed by the 1,000ft aerial masts around it – this must be the only trig point with an inferiority complex. The masts themselves seem strangely comfortable in their surroundings and at least one local said that they would be missed if removed. But be careful when you walk near them in winter – a sign warns you to keep an eye open for falling ice, and when you consider from what height it might have fallen, these are wise words indeed.

Winter Hill was the site of the first mass walking trespass, which took place in 1896, 36 years before the more famous march at Kinder Scout. The then landowner, Colonel Ainsworth of Smithills Hall, closed the moor to protect his grouse shooting interests, and 8,000 people decided to encourage him to change his mind.

The Route

Distance: 8.9km/5 1/2 miles
Start: *There are numerous routes to and across Winter Hill. Park south of Belmont (SD676156), head west to Winter Hill. Head north to trig point then north west to Hordern Stoops. Pick up footpath heading east back to Belmont.*

Before you go...

Stay here

Black Dog, Belmont

There are plenty of places to stay around the edges of the West Pennine Moors. The towns of Blackburn, Accrington, Darwen, Rawtenstall, Bury, Bolton, Horwich and Chorley dot the perimeter of the West Pennine Moors, with Manchester and the motorways just a few miles to the south. However, Perry had the good fortune of knocking on the door of the Black Dog pub, on Church Street in the central West Pennine village of Belmont.

Not only does it serve scrumptious tucker (Wednesday to Sunday), but it also has a handful of rooms for weary walkers. The pub dates from the mid 18th century and serves excellent value, outstanding real ale from the local brewer Holts. History buffs might like to pop to the road junction, outside the Black Dog, where a fountain recalls Queen Victoria's diamond jubilee of 1897.

For booking information call 01204 811218.

Northcote Manor

Northcote Road, Langho,
Blackburn,
Lancashire BB6 8BE,
Tel 01254 240555,
www.northcotemanor.com

Visit this

Turton Tower

Turton Tower, near Bolton, is perfect for afternoons when you want to rest weary thighs. It has various rooms laid out as they would have been in centuries past, including a bedroom with furniture designed by William Morris. The tower itself was first built in about 1420. Since then, several owners (including both sides of the Civil War) have added to and altered several aspects of the design.

Opening times vary – call 01204 852203 for details.

Further information

For more information about the West Pennine Moors visit www.lancashirehillcountry.co.uk or call Blackburn tourist information centre on 01254 53277.

Maps

Ordnance Survey Explorer 287

A taste of Lancashire

Lancashire hotpot

So you have sampled our hotpot of Lancashire walks, now it's time to eat the real thing. Celebrity chef Nigel Howarth, of Northcote Manor, Langho, Blackburn, is famous for his Lancashire hotpot, which he serves with oyster beignet and spiced red cabbage. Indeed, he is so passionate about the local speciality that he has just had a new Aga oven fitted that will slow-cook the dishes in the traditional manner. You can enjoy one of these delicious meals on your walking tour of the West Pennines, but be sure to give Nigel at least four hours' notice, because his hotpots need this much time to be cooked properly.

Call 01254 240555 to make your reservation.

Alternatively, if you fancy making your own hotpot, follow our recipe here.

(Serves 3-4)
Middle neck of lamb, cut into 8 chops
4 lamb kidneys
2lb potatoes
8oz onion
8oz carrots
3oz butter
1/2 pint stock
Herbs, bay-leaf, salt and pepper to taste

1 Trim excess fat off the lamb and fry until brown in some butter. Place herbs in bottom of a casserole dish and arrange the chops with the kidneys (sliced), onions and carrots (both peeled and chopped). Season well.

2 Pour in the stock. Top the mixture with layers of sliced potatoes and brush liberally with melted butter. Cover and cook gently in a medium oven for two hours.

3 Take the lid off and brown for 20 minutes (if your dish is flame-proof, you could do this under a grill). Serve with broccoli, carrots, pickled red cabbage or other seasonal vegetables of your choice.

Black pudding

No walking tour of the West Pennines would be complete without sampling a local delicacy. The award-winning black pudding of Andrew Holt's RS Ireland, at Waterfoot, is lauded in this country and abroad. Indeed, to complement the already creaking awards cabinet Andrew has in his offices at RS Ireland, he has just been made a chevalier de goute boudin noir – or 'knight of the black pudding'. Most of us know black pudding as a breakfast dish, but there are many other culinary uses for it, including as an ingredient in the traditional Lancashire hotpot.

For more information, or to visit RS Ireland, call 01706 224990.

Chorley cake

If hotpots and black puddings aren't your cup of tea, we suggest you head to Chorley, 10 miles north west of Bolton. Here you will find another local delicacy – Chorley cakes. Made using dried fruit, they're similar to Eccles cakes and are believed to date back to medieval times. Back then, they were looked upon as a convenience food, because they provided a neatly-packaged, satisfying snack. Today, you can find various recipes at bakeries around Chorley – the recipes for which are often closely guarded secrets!

Happy returns

In 2004 the Yorkshire Dales celebrates its golden jubilee as a national park. What better time to explore this walkers' paradise?

It's not often that we get to celebrate a golden jubilee. But with the Queen's in 2002, the 50th anniversary of the ascent of Mount Everest in 2003 and a particularly walker-resonant jubilee to take place in 2004 we have, like buses, three coming along at once. For 2004 sees the 50th anniversary of the Yorkshire Dales National Park.

To celebrate, we have revisited the Dales to remind ourselves just why the area deserves to be a national park. We teamed up with some old friends, and made some new ones, on an adventure that took in classic routes and a number of newer trails.

Many of us first discovered the beauty of the Dales through watching the TV series All Creatures Great And Small. The Dales has now repaid its favourite son with the Herriot Way, and we teamed up with the real-life son of James Herriot, Jim Wight, for a walk on the Swaledale section of the route, and some tales of veterinary misadventure.

The Abbeys Amble is a new 103-mile route that can be completed in one go or, through some clever designing, in a series of day-long circular walks. It's a fascinating history hike that takes in some of the UK's finest abbeys and castles.

You don't really get much more 'classic' than Malham Cove. This stunning place was being heralded long before the national park was even a twinkle in a Minister's eye. It's such a classic walking location that the Dales National Park Authority has set it up as one of its 50th anniversary walks.

Wensleydale

Above: On the Pennine Way north of Hardraw, on a zig-zag route back to Hawes.

Below: The Green Dragon, with Hardraw Force out back

"There's more to a cowpat than meets the eye," says Mark Reid as we head out from Hawes. It's just one of the Inn Way author's pearls of wisdom as we accompany him on a route he's devised for the Brasher 'Boots and Beer' Festival. The festival brings together the sublime combination of superb walks and great pubs in the Dales. Mark is in charge of working out 12 walks, and we're helping him to recce just one of them today. Despite being, as a local might put it, from the wrong side of the Pennines, Lancastrian Mark is the ideal man for the job, because the Dales are his 'local'. Best of all, Mark has written a guide to the area and its pubs, making him an expert in all fields, so to speak. We learn that butterflies drink from the top of cowpats and stone barns have a double-walled construction.

Mark, Perry and I set off from Hawes, a lively market town at the heart of upper Wensleydale, then head through the village of Sedbusk before a steep ascent takes us up towards Lovely Seat. The climb isn't initially repaid, as we walk through mist on the top, barely able to see the golden plovers flying just a few metres ahead of us. But when we

stop at a cairn the haze clears, and we see the whole of the valley spread out beneath us, forming the distinctive Dales patchwork of fields and drystone walls. We see the sunlight flit across the valley, occasionally hovering to bathe some of the fields in light while others remain dark and forbidding. The effect is like film on fast-forward, as clouds pass along the valley, making way for sun at a second's notice. "There are so many shades of green," says Mark admiring the view.

Heading along the ridge we are surrounded by classic Dales scenery, the kind that, oddly, seems instantly familiar. We pass shake holes – limestone formations that have subsided with the rain into strange pits – and head down to the road, letting our feet run away under us as we gallop through fields of wildflowers, before reaching the Butter Tubs Road, which gets its name from particularly deep shake holes that seem to disappear into the bowels of the earth. We turn off to Hardraw for lunch before we reach the tubs.

The village is home to the highest waterfall in the UK, Hardraw Force. The waterfall is privately

> *"The waterfall is privately owned and sits at the back of a pub, making this quite a beer garden."*

owned and sits at the back of a pub, making this quite a beer garden. The falls are impressively high and powerful. Signs warn that it is dangerous to walk behind the waterfall, although Kevin Costner did, when he showered there in the film Robin Hood, Prince Of Thieves. After a misty start the weather's starting to hot up, and the thought of a refreshing shower is tempting. But there are no volunteers to recreate Costner's naked dive. In any case, the risk of falling rocks makes it too dangerous, so we settle for wandering on the stones in front of the waterfall.

One leisurely lunch later, Mark leads us up to the Pennine Way, as we follow a zig-zag route across Wensleydale. This long-distance route is one of three that pass through this area, including the Dales Way and the Coast-to-Coast walk. Perhaps that's why the few walkers we meet on the way seem especially friendly, stopping to ask for directions, or offering to take our photographer's camera to capture all of us on film.

After a final climb on to the stony path, it's a straightforward route back down to Appersett and across the fields to Hawes. The boots element of the day well and truly covered, all that now remains is to sample the beer.

The Route

Boots and Beer route

Distance: *17km/11 miles.*

Time: *3-4 hours.*

Terrain: *Mostly good clear paths. One steep ascent.*

Route: *From Hawes (grid ref SD8789) follow the Pennine Way north, leaving the trail to take the right fork towards Sedbusk. From here climb Shutt Lane, then head up to Pike Hill, descending on the footpath to Butter Tubs Road. Take the first footpath on your right into Simonstone, taking a brief detour to Hardraw Force, before following the Pennine Way back to Hawes.*

Map: *Ordnance Survey Landranger 98*

Mark Reid considers showing us his Kevin Costner impression .

Abbeys Amble

Following in the footsteps of 12th-century friars

"The sound of traffic is gradually replaced by the music of oystercatchers and the soft tinkling percussion of the Ure's stone-splashing flow."

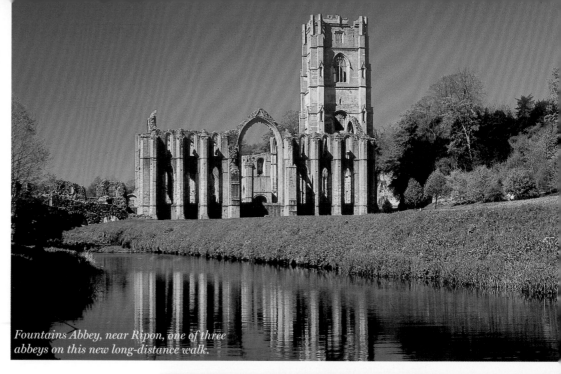

Fountains Abbey, near Ripon, one of three abbeys on this new long-distance walk.

It's a rare day indeed that I am consumed with a calling for monastic life – 'rare' as in almost entirely non-existent, and usually 'cured' with a couple of pints down the local and a flutter on the geegees.

But today I have to admit some admiration for our be-habited brothers. For today I am walking the Abbeys Amble – or part of it, at least. Despite myself (and despite the rather twee name of this new long-distance walk) I am thoroughly enjoying this 'pilgrimage' in the footsteps of our forefather friars.

I'm in Masham, to the east of the national park, and I'm walking the banks of the River Ure, which at one time lent its name to the dale through which it flows. But 'Uredale' was dropped when the village of Wensley experienced something of a Middle Age boom, and 'Wensleydale' has stuck since. I'm heading for Jervaulx Abbey, which was built close to the Ure by Cistercian monks in 1156 and takes its own name from the Norman French for 'Ure Vale'.

Jervaulx is one of three abbeys on the 103-mile Abbeys Amble, the others being Fountains Abbey near Ripon, and Bolton Abbey. But to make up for the rather poor abbey-to-mileage ratio on this walk, the AA, as it describes itself in the guidebook, also takes in three castles – Bolton, Middleham and Ripley.

There are three castles to be admired on the Abbeys Amble – this is Bolton.

After Jervaulx I'm pushing on to Middleham, the one-time powerbase of Richard III. So Masham to Middleham, via Jervaulx Abbey – 101-2 miles of, as it turns out, walking bliss.

If truth be known, it was a little difficult to pull myself away from the market town of Masham this morning. The place is stuffed full of antiquity, and one could easily while away a day here, walking the streets and squares in admiration of this charming town.

For instance, in the churchyard at Masham stands the remains of a carved eighth-century Anglo Saxon cross, which goes some way to demonstrating the pedigree of this ancient Yorkshire community. In medieval times, the town had its own 'peculiar', or church, court and this is remembered today through the name of a locally brewed ale – we are all familiar with Theakston Old Peculiar. Today Masham is also home to Paul Theakston's Black Sheep Brewery, and a tour of this traditional brew-house is a must for anyone interested in the craft of hops, yeast and fermentation.

But as I pick up the riverside footpath that drops away from Masham's bridge, and the sound of traffic is gradually replaced by the music of oystercatchers and the soft tinkling percussion of the Ure's stone-splashing flow, I feel my heart beating just a little faster with the anticipation of what's to come.

You know it's funny, but no matter how many times I step out on a new walk, the child in me is enthused with a sense of adventure, and I have to control the urge not to skip through the grass.

I allow a broad smile to creep across my face. It's a beautiful late-summer day, armadas of mallards make busy manoeuvres on the brandy-brown water to my right, wildflowers set the pastures ahead ablaze with colour, nonchalant Yorkshire sheep stare vacantly at me, displaying no emotion at my intrusion other than to squat down and relieve themselves as I pass – their way, no doubt, of expressing exactly what they think of such two-legged impropriety.

The river drops away now and I find myself on a plateau above it, sweeping orange and yellow fields now hidden by cool and shading wooded stretches, wild woodland violets and aristocratic foxgloves dance in the revitalising breeze. On the far side of the bank, Clifton Castle appears out of the trees, magnificent and forbidding. More fields, more sheep, the river looping off on some ox-bow mission all of its own, and I emerge suddenly from a tree-lined boulevard for a country lane and the gates of Jervaulx Park.

What constantly surprises on these history walks is the very real – it seems to me – presence of our forefathers. Jervaulx Abbey, destroyed by Henry VIII during the dissolution of the monasteries, is about 1,000 years old. Crumbling and enchantingly overgrown, it looks every bit its age. Yet the sensation that washes over me when treading its paths and now-grassy chambers is of all the people who have inhabited and enjoyed it, and continue to do so. In some ways it is a strangely humbling experience, but humbling in a comforting way, like attending a large family reunion.

After Jervaulx, footpath and river come together again for the shortish push to Middleham. At Ulshaw I take the path on the northern bank, west for some stepping stones, then head up a bank in the opposite direction, across a series of rising fields. At the top there is a stile and, when I look ahead from this vantage point, I can make out a flag on the top of a castle turret fluttering in the breeze. When Jervaulx's monks travelled this way to Richard III's Middleham it must have appeared exactly the same.

But if kings and monks are the star of today's walk, tomorrow it is the turn of a country vet.

The Route

Jervaulx Abbey and Middleham Castle
Distance: *17km/11 miles.*
Time: *3-4 hours.*
Terrain: *Mostly riverside footpath.*
Route: *From Masham pick up footpath at bridge (grid ref SE226812) and head north to High Mains Farm. Head west to Low Ellington, then north to Kilgram Bridge (SE191860). Follow lane to Jervaulx Park and head through. Pick up footpath to riverbank (SE167858) and head west. Cross river at Ulshaw and head west until Stepping Stones. Head north west to Middleham Castle.*
Map: *Ordnance Survey Landranger 99*

Doorways to the past – Perry and Marianne explore Jervaulx

The Herriot Way

It should happen to a walker

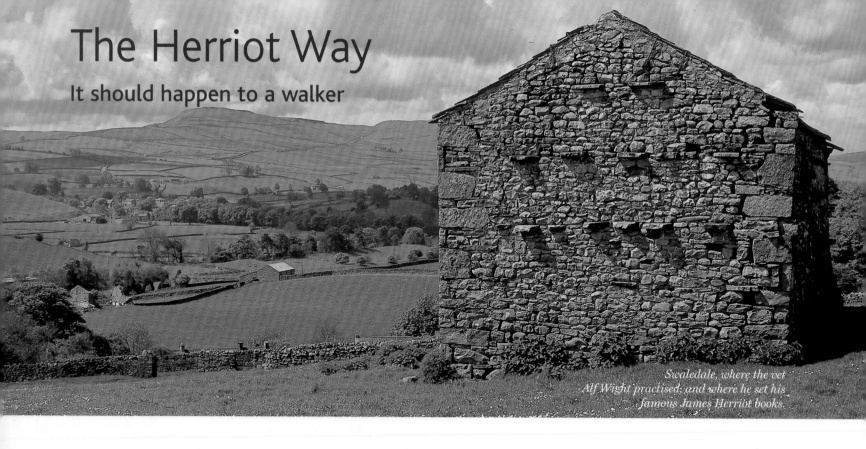

Swaledale, where the vet Alf Wight practised; and where he set his famous James Herriot books.

There are few actors who have been as strongly identified with their role as Christopher Timothy, who became known for his portrayal of James Herriot on screen and, specifically, for shoving his arm up the rear end of a cow – no stunt vets involved. By the same token, few writers have been identified so strongly with a region as James Herriot has with the Yorkshire Dales.

The real Herriot was the late Alf Wight, whose best-selling tales, based on his time as a vet in the small town of Thirsk, have been translated into 20 languages. Today we are lucky enough to be walking with Jim Wight, the son of Alf/James. Like his dad, he was a vet and, as we walk, he entertains us with his natural gift for story-telling, something else that seems to have been passed down.

Many of his stories revolve around the peculiarities of the Yorkshire character. He tells us of the occasion when he spent a long night delivering piglets in the backyard of a pub. "You must be ready for a drink," said the landlady when he'd finally finished. Jim gratefully accepted. "That'll be one and six," said the canny Yorkshire woman.

Jim lives in an enviable location between the Dales and the Moors, but it's the Dales that are his favourite, and he's been a fan since the days when he went walking with his father and sister. He continues to be a keen walker, with the mountains of Scotland a close favourite behind the Yorkshire Dales. Today, though, we've persuaded him away from the high tops to join us for a walk in the valley of Swaledale, where he explains some of the history behind the area.

This was a lead mining area in the 19th century, and was well inhabited until the supplies within reach were exhausted, and the market collapsed. Since then the valley has been far quieter than its bustling neighbour, Wensleydale, although it is just as beautiful. Today it is illuminated by the sun and is looking its shiny Sunday best.

"The miners used to walk for miles to get to work," says Jim. "Imagine having to leave behind this sunshine to go into the dark mines."

Our path offers views of the river below and the hills above, some still scarred by their mining past. We pass simple stone barns, protected by law from the twin threats of destruction and conversion.

The route we're taking forms part of the Herriot Way, a trail that links four youth hostels that Jim and his father walked between in the 1950s. The route also takes in locations used in the TV series, such as the charming village of Askrigg, which stood in for Darrowby, in turn the pseudonym of Thirsk.

We head back on the path that leads us next to the River Swale, which gives the valley its name. There can be no doubt that James Herriot has helped to make this area even more popular, a fact brought home to us as Jim relates one of the many anecdotes from his dad's books. In this, the hapless Tristan mixes up two parcels, sending a package of ointment to a lab for testing, and a sample of faeces to a farmer to apply to one of his cows. A walker just in front of us, who has no reason to know of

Jim's connection, drinks in the tale before turning to say, "That's one of my favourite stories, too."

Jim tells us some tales of his own time living in Yorkshire, like the time a friend went to buy a dozen eggs. On returning home she found there were only 11, and resolved to take it up with the farmer next time they met. When she did, she put it to the farmer that there was one less egg in the box than there should have been. "Aye," said the farmer, "but one of them was a double yolker." Jim laughs, and says with semi-incredulity, "Only in Yorkshire!"

Jim has travelled worldwide to speak to the readers of his father's books. He says they all identify with the stories, despite the fact that the setting is entirely distinctive – apparently farmers are the same the world over. It is this universal recognition of the characters that has ensured the books' success, just as the special Dales scenery adds an extra something to the stories.

At the end of our walk we head back towards Askrigg. Jim stops us briefly at a high pass, where the whole of Swaledale is visible. "I used to bring my father up here when he was ill," he tells us. "It was one of his favourite places." The beauty of the landscape provides a moving testament to a son's love for his father, and a family's love of the Dales. Tomorrow shall bring an equally celebrated landscape.

Top: Jim and Marianne on the banks of the River Swale.
Left: Askrigg House stood in for James Herriot's TV surgery

"...the sun was dazzling and the long green line of the fells rose before me, thrusting exultantly into a sky of summer blue..."

James Herriot, Vets Might Fly

The Route

Herriot Trail Swaledale circular
Distance: *9.7km/6 miles.*
Time: *21/2 hours.*
Terrain: *Easy, gentle paths.*
Route: *From Gunnerside (grid ref SD9598) take the top path that leads towards Muker, following this all the way along. To return follow the lower path next to the river, which occasionally intersects your outward route.*
Map: *Ordnance Survey Landranger 98*

Malham Cove

A classic Dales walk for a special celebration

The shards of sunlight that dance off Malham Beck lend the water a suitably golden hue for a 50th anniversary walk. For that is why Marianne and I are here – to walk a Dales classic in celebration of the national park's golden jubilee.

The waterfall at Gordale Scar – geology at its most wild and dramatic.

But where to find such a route in all of the Dales? Well, if there is one location that has been celebrated far longer than the mere half century that the national park has been around, it is Malham Cove and its environs, which count such august historical figures as John Ruskin, Turner, Rev Charles Kingsley, William Wordsworth and WH Auden among its admirers.

And when you get to Malham Cove you can see why. But first, under the principle of leaving the best until last, Marianne and I are walking away from the cove, along the banks of Malham Beck, at the start of a circular walk that will take in an enchanted cave and waterfall, a vast roofless cavern, a glacial lake and a singular limestone 'pavement' that is like stepping on the cracked epidermis of the Earth herself.

We ford the beck near the visitor centre, glad we had the foresight to wax our boots before our adventure, and find ourselves on the Pennine Way, itself a piece of walking history, being the first national trail to criss-cross this island of ours. But before we have time to appreciate the shade from the sycamores that line the banks of the beck running parallel to our path, or admire the courage of the dippers that wheel above our heads warbling warning cries to kith and kin, we reach Mires Barn and head left, a sign pointing the way to the first of our Yorkshire treats.

Janet's Foss is an intimate rocky amphitheatre bejewelled with mossy oaks, and with a crystal clear pool and thundering waterfall at centre stage. It is located at the end of a leafy trail, in a wood owned by The National Trust.

'Foss' is the old Norse word for waterfall, or force, and Janet, so the story goes, is the queen of the fairies who lives behind this watery cascade. Fairy queen or not, Janet is obviously a successful individual, for she has a second home, Janet's Cave, beneath a lip in the wall on the other side of the pool. We leave this watery idyll and head up and out into sunlight, a country lane stretching ahead to the north east. We pass Gordale Bridge and take a left into Gordale Gorge, impressive, sheer limestone cliffs rising claustrophobically either side of us, a lone kestrel hovering silently above. The genteel path underfoot belies the rugged landscape to be found at the end of the gorge, for Gordale Scar is a manifestation of geology at its most wild and dramatic.

> "Fairy queen or not, Janet is obviously a successful individual, for she has a second home, beneath a lip in the wall on the other side of the pool."

Limestone all around on the Pennine Way, above Malham Cove.

What once was a great cavern with high vaulted ceiling, is now a deep cleft in the earth, the roof having collapsed, leaving sheer walls that overhang and a series of waterfalls, one of which flows through a circular gap in the side of the limestone cliff. Adventurous walkers can scramble up and through the gorge for a path that heads north west to Malham Tarn, but Marianne and I return to the bridge, for a route that heads west across Cawden Flats. The views are stunning.

Malham Tarn was granted to the monks of Fountains Abbey in the 12th century by William de Percy, and today is still considered excellent for trout fishing. There are also plenty of water birds to be admired here – curlews, great-crested grebes and mallards. But Marianne and I are impatient to get on, and we pick up the Pennine Way again, heading south on the final leg of our walk. At Comb Hill we begin to get an inkling of the geological treat to come, exposed limestone creating a deepish gorge, from which we emerge on to a vast flat area of deeply fissured limestone that stretches to a sheer 80m drop to the valley floor. We hop-scotch to the edge and stand at the very top of Malham Cove – the whole of England in the palm of our hands.

The local peregrines are staying hidden today. But the evening light, with its golden shards, makes up for their loss on this, our Dales anniversary walk.

Dwarfed by the 80m walls of Malham Cove.

On foot for Janet's Foss, an enchanting Dales waterfall.

The Route

Malham Cove
Dales Golden Jubilee Walk
Terrain: *Mostly limestone footpath.*
Route: *From visitor centre (grid ref SD901637) cross beck and head south on Pennine Way to Mires Barn (SD902624). Pick up footpath heading north east to Janet's Foss. At Gordale Bridge, take path west, then north, to tarn. Return via Malham Cove on the Pennine Way. Map: Ordnance Survey Landranger 98*
Distance: *10.5km/6½ miles.*
Time: *3-4 hours.*

Stiles aplenty between Malham Tarn and Malham Cove.

Before you go...

Visit here

Wensleydale Creamery
An essential stop for fans of this tasty, crumbly cheese, which is hand-made here in the valley. See Wensleydale being made, taste it, then buy some in the shop if it takes your fancy.
Wensleydale Dairy Products Ltd,
Gayle Lane, Hawes,
North Yorkshire DL8 3RN.
Tel: 01969 667664.
Visit: www.wensleydale.co.uk

Black Sheep Brewery
In 1992 the family brewing business that made Theakston bitter was taken over. Paul Theakston, the former managing director, responded by setting up the Black Sheep Brewery. Since its launch it has gone from strength to strength, raising the production of beer from 50 to 950 barrels each week. It now makes a staggering 11 million pints a year, with four different types of beer on offer. The brewery offers tours of the site, as well as meals in its own bistro.
Black Sheep Brewery,
Wellgarth, Masham,
Ripon, North Yorkshire HG4 4EN.
Tel: 01765 689227.
Visit: www.blacksheepbrewery.com

Stay here

Cocketts Hotel, Hawes
A Grade II listed 17th-century building that's been converted into a small, comfortable hotel on the main street at Hawes. Great walks are readily accessible from here.
Tel:01969 667312
www.cocketts.co.uk

Bank Villa, Masham
A friendly B&B with a lovely hilltop garden. Also within easy walking (or staggering) distance of the Black Sheep Brewery.
Tel: 01765 689605
www.bankvilla.com

More Information

Tourist information: Call 01904 707070 to request a walking pack, which can be tailored to your requirements.
www.walkyorkshire.com (general information about walking throughout the county).

Pirates, poetry & paths

Join us for tales of saints, sinners, heroes and villains...oh, and stop-you-in-your stride views.

Words: **Perry Cleveland-Peck, Karen Pereczes** Pictures: **Matthew Roberts**

What is it about west Wales that so inspires mankind? The wizard Merlin, the brains behind Arthur's brawn, is said to be imprisoned here to this day. The blue stones of Stonehenge were hewn out of the Preseli hills here and carried to Somerset – nobody knows why. Some of the most forbidding seafarers were born in Pembrokeshire or learnt their ropes around its shores. And one of the world's finest writers, Welsh poet Dylan Thomas walked this county's footpaths, capturing them in his poems and prose.

We have gone to Pembrokeshire to rejoice in the footpaths that for over 50 years now have been open to all, and to walk in the footsteps of the county's heroes. We visited three locations on the 186-mile coast path, a trinity of microcosms on this three-sided coastline.

In the north we visited Fishguard and walked east to Dinas Head in the footsteps of Dylan Thomas, with the creator of the poet's trail. In the south, we walked from Stack Rocks to Lydstep Point, in memory of the Pembrokeshire pirates – sailors credited with founding the US Navy and even the Jamaican accent. And in the west, we walked simply to celebrate the 50 colourful years of the Pembrokeshire Path itself, from Abereiddi and its famous Blue Lagoon to St Justinian with its bright red lifeboat station. We loved it. We hope you do too.

Fishguard

Find inspiration – just like
Dylan Thomas – in sleepy
'Llareggub'.

Above: Looking out to sea from Dinas Island at the end of the walk.

It is something of a struggle to visit west Wales and not to come across at least some reference to the country's favourite literary son, the poet Dylan Thomas.

Which is why I'm standing on the quay-side of Fishguard's Lower Town, in preparation for a walk in Dylan Thomas' footsteps. Now Fishguard was known to Thomas. His biographer, David Thomas (no relation), records that Dylan travelled here with his wife, Caitlin, and friends in 1936 for the Eisteddfod music festival, and no doubt he visited Fishguard on other occasions. But this Pembrokeshire port's picturesque Lower Town was also the location for Andrew Sinclair's 1972 film of Under Milk Wood, starring Richard Burton, Elizabeth Taylor and Peter O'Toole. And while I have never been here before, the place seems familiar to me from my memory of this fine British movie adaptation.

"We are descending now, black sheep in the fields to our right, white horses crashing onto the rocks beneath us to our left."

Thomas' Under Milk Wood, published posthumously in 1954, is set in the make-believe Welsh fishing village of Llareggub, and tells the tale of its sleepy inhabitants, as narrated by the blind Captain Cat. But what Llareggub (try reading it backwards) lacks in excitement, its Fishguard stand-in more than makes up for in wonderful Welsh walking opportunities. As I look out across

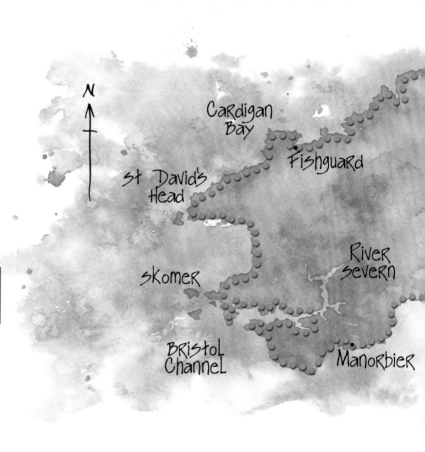

the harbour to the "sloeback, slow, black, crowblack, fishingboat-bobbing sea" and listen for the "dew falling, and the hushed town breathing" it strikes me that I couldn't have chosen a better place to start this walk.

Or a more informed person to share at least part of the walk with. For just a short way up the coast, past the 18th-century Fishguard Fort, is the village of Pwllgwaelod and The Old Sailors restaurant, where the Dylan Thomas biographer David Thomas and his partner and I plan to rendezvous for a walk and a chat. The Old Sailors, which sits on the characteristic grey-sand foreshore of Pwllgwaelod beach, was once called The Sailors Safety pub, and it was here that Dylan came to eat with friends just two years before he died.

"Dylan made a lot of visits to places that are now all on the Pembrokeshire Coast Path," says David, when we meet up. "He often took visitors to St David's Head and to the cathedral there. In the summer of 1951, he took two Americans on a tour of Pembrokeshire. They went first to St David's and then to Newgale, where they visited the Duke of Edinburgh pub – maybe it has a new name today? – and Caitlin bathed naked in the sea. They then came here to Pwllgwaelod and Dinas Head, to have a lobster supper at the Sailors Safety, and this is still a great place to go for seafood and drinks."

We set off up the steepish path for Pen-y-fan, the viewpoint on the most northerly tip of the peninsular that shares its name, if not its altitude, with the highest mountain in the Brecon Beacons. The last of the year's bracken lends a thick organic aroma to the air, the rolling Irish sea that fills the horizon is at once a peppermint grey-green and deep blue hue with the passing, scudding, windblown clouds above.

"The other point about Dylan," says David, looking back to the mainland and, on the distant skyline, the silhouette of west Wales' most famous mountain, Carn Ingli, "is that he was an obsessive walker, from his schooldays. He enjoyed walking as a way of meeting people in the countryside. But it was while walking that he composed his poems and stories."

We are descending now, black sheep in the fields to our right, white horses crashing onto the rocks beneath us to our left, until we reach a short wooded section, hawthorn reaching skywards, dense save for a narrow corridor that twists and drops in steps. We emerge at Cwm-yr-eglwys and its 12th-century church of St Brynach. Only the belfry and the west wall remain of this church, the rest destroyed in a storm in 1859. But it is an atmospheric spot, the sea crashing on the shore a few feet away, the air filled with salty spray. And as evening approaches we pause for a while to remember the poet Dylan Thomas, and listen for the "dew falling and the hushed town breathing".

The Route

Dylan Thomas Walk
Distance: *12km/71/2 miles.*
Terrain: *Pavement, then coastal footpath. Some steps.*
Route: *From Fishguard Lower Town (grid ref SM963372) pick up coast path and head east. The 412 Richards Brothers bus leaves Dinas Cross bus stop at 09.42 - then every hour at 42 mins past the hour until 18.42, Monday to Saturday.*
Map: Ordnance Survey Explorer OL35, Landranger 157.
Time: *3 hours.*

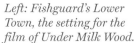

Left: Fishguard's Lower Town, the setting for the film of Under Milk Wood.

Manorbier

The Draught above Smugglers Cave at Lydstep Caverns – ideal for hiding pirates' booty.

A life lived in fear is a life half-lived, I tell myself, as I nervously approach the 'man over cliff' warning sign. I peek over the edge at the sea below, waves crashing on to jagged boulders, and inhale the air and saltwater spray. The terrain is wild, dangerous, and breathtakingly beautiful.

I'm walking the south Pembrokeshire Coast Path with Country Walking's Nicola and my 14-month-old daughter, Eocha. And today we are in search of Pembrokeshire's pirates.

Ahead of us is Stack Rocks, and we pause for a fantastic aerobatic display, guillemots performing freefalling spirals in the spray. Stack Rocks is also known as Elegug Stacks – 'elegug' being the Welsh word for guillemot. Two pillars of detached limestone are home to colonies of these classic seabirds, as well as fulmar petrels, razorbills and many gulls.

To our west is a stretch of coastline that to this day still suffers at the hands of warmongering seafarers, albeit those of a more modern variety – the coastline is permanently closed due to unexploded missiles. But a notice ahead tells us that the path to the east is open – there is no firing at the Castlemartin range today.

Clinging to the cliffs of the secluded headland ahead is a sixth-century Celtic hermitage, founded when St Govan hid in a rocky fissure to escape from Pembrokeshire's pirates. Thankful for his life, he built a chapel on that very spot.

Nobody knows St Govan's true identity. Some say he was Sir Gawain, King Arthur's nephew and a Knight of the Round Table, while others say he was an Irish abbot, St Gobham.

I attempt to count the steep, uneven steps underfoot that legend says number differently down and up. I tally 72 as I descend. No doubt the number will change on my return.

St Govan's Head is Pembrokeshire's most southern point. On a clear day it offers views of Devon and Cornwall, the Gower Peninsula and Lundy Island. Below is New Quay, a favourite pirate landing spot. A cargo of spirits smuggled from here in 1833 was carried off in bags on horseback and distributed locally – reminding me of the film Whisky Galore. Are we getting closer with our quest?

At Broad Haven beach, with its spectacular Church Rock, I can't help looking to the horizon and wondering how it must have felt to be out on the high seas during the golden age of piracy, living in fear of pirates such as Pembrokeshire-born Bartholomew Roberts, aka 'Black Bart', one of the most successful and menacing pirates ever.

In his time, Bart captured 400 ships and collected £80 million of treasure. But he is better remembered as the originator of the universal pirate emblem – the skull and crossbones. Because he wore a red coat, the French called him 'Le Joli Rouge', which was corrupted to Jolly Roger by the English, and eventually became associated with the flag, rather than the person.

A little further down the coast and we reach the village of Manorbier. Gerald of Wales, a writer, historian and ecclesiastic who was born in Manorbier Castle in 1146, described this area as, "The pleasantest spot in Wales," and I have to agree with his sentiment, if not his grammar. As I walk past the Neolithic cromlech known as King's Quoit to Priest's Nose, it's easy to understand why this spot has a long history as a sacred place. The landscape is powerful and dramatic, and exudes an energy that has inspired men and women

The Route

Pirates Walk
Distance: 25.3km/153/4 miles.
Time: 6 hours.
Terrain: Mostly cliff paths, moorland trails and beaches. Some steps.
Route: From Elugag Rocks (grid ref SR925946) pick up coast path and head east. The winter Coastal Cruiser bus runs on Tuesdays, Thursdays and Saturdays.
Map: Ordnance Survey Explorer OL36, Landranger 158.

throughout the ages, people such as Virginia Woolf, who wrote 'The Waves' during her time here.

After the turquoise waters of Precipe Bay the path goes inland. Nicola, Eocha and I continue to Skrinkle Haven, where fingers of carboniferous limestone and old red sandstone rock, with its natural arches known as the Church Doors, stretch across golden sand to dip into the sea. Fulmars and razorbills nest on these cliffs, while gulls noisily catch the breeze.

After the spectacular vertical beds of limestone at Skomer, and its Iron Age fort, the path descends steeply down a gorge to Lydstep Caverns. Here, a great blowhole called Draught provided access to Smugglers Cave. As it is low tide, we clamber down to explore inside. The rock formations are a higgledy-piggledy mix of giant molar teeth and reaching spires that surround hollow caverns.

Looking out to sea from Lydstep Point is Caldey Island, where Cistercian monks continue a tradition of prayer and peaceful living that began in Celtic times. But the island has a lesser known, more violent past...smugglers hid booty in Cathedral Caves, and Caldey was a refuge for this area's most notorious freebooter, John Paul Jones, and his fantastically named look-out Leekie Porridge.

Jones, a ruthless marauding pirate akin to Blackbeard, was born in Scotland and is credited by some as being the founder of the US Navy. He regularly moored up at Caldey to take on water, anchoring in what is still known today as Paul Jones Bay. It is said that when he died in 1792, his body was pushed into a crevice in the rocks near Ord Point.

Captain Henry Morgan, whose name today is forever linked with bottles of rum, also hid out on Caldey Island. Born around 1635 in Monmouthshire, this Welshman sailed as a privateer, though his behaviour was, at times, more like that of a mercenary. In 1671, when returning from plundering the city of Panama, he left most of his faithful followers behind, without ships or food, slipping off in the night with most of the booty to Jamaica. Towards the end of his life, Henry Morgan was said to have bought an estate in Jamaica, and the Welsh accent is credited by some as being the origin of today's Caribbean accent.

Nowadays, fishing and pleasure boats have taken the place of sloops and schooners. But, for me, this part of Pembrokeshire, with its secret caves and coves, will always be remembered as the Pirate Path.

Entrance to smugglers cove

"Bart collected £80 million of treasure. But he is better remembered as the originator of the pirate emblem – the skull and crossbones."

Nicola and Karen at the entrance to Smugglers Cave.

St Davids Head

Too much for French invaders, but great for walkers

The Route

Anniversary Walk
Distance: 17km/10 1/2 miles.
Time: 4 hours.
Terrain: Mostly cliff paths, moorland trails and beaches. Some steps.
Route: From the Blue Lagoon (grid ref SM796315) pick up coast path and head west. The 'Strumble Shuttle' bus in St David's runs Mondays, Thursdays and Saturdays between St David's and Porthgain (just east of Abereiddy).
Map: Ordnance Survey Explorer OL35, Landranger 157.

Just over 200 years ago, four French warships anchored off Carreg Wastad, to the east of St David's on the coastline. Some 1,400 Napoleonic soldiers, many of them ex-convicts, invaded this remote Welsh headland and took control of a nearby farmhouse, ready to do battle against the Brits.

The details of the next two days are sketchy. One local cobbler, a Jemima Nicholas, is said to have captured 12 of the French with nothing but a pitchfork, an action for which she was awarded a life pension. And folklore has it that a group of Welsh women, dressed in the traditional red shawls and tall black hats of the time, were mistaken by the French for a British army division, and scared off. Whatever the case, it is certainly true that just 48 hours after the invasion, the French surrendered en masse at nearby Goodwick Sands. What this says about French men or, for that matter, Welsh women, I will leave to you, dear reader. But mainland Britain has not been invaded since.

This is not the only current Pembrokeshire anniversary worth noting. Half a century ago, in 1953, the same year in

to community en route. It has also created 52 circular walks, all of which touch upon the coast path.

Country Walking's Nicola, photographer Matthew and I are walking one of these routes, on the western edge of the coast, near St David's.

We started our walk just after breakfast at Abereiddy, up the coast. During the 19th and early 20th centuries this coastal community played an important role in slate production. The industry has long gone now – all that's left are the remains of a few workers' cottages and buildings, plus a dark flooded quarry known locally as the Blue Lagoon. The lagoon, and the craggy foreshore around it, make for a diverting place to beachcombe and rock-pool for half an hour or so.

Between Abereiddy and St David's Head lie a series of rocky tors that offer dramatic, if undulating, views over the sea to the north, bruised and irritable in the blustery winds today. These hard igneous tors – from east to west, Penberi, Carn Treliwyd, Carn Prefedd, Carnedd Lleithr and Carn

Below: St Justinian's distinctive red lifeboat station.

fact that the poet Dylan Thomas died, the Pembrokeshire Coast Path National Trail came into existence. And 2002 marked the golden jubilee of the Pembrokeshire Coast National Park itself. So walkers the world over have every reason to wish Pembrokeshire many happy returns, and have no excuse not to return themselves.

To mark these anniversaries, the national park authority has, among other celebratory events and activities, run a relay walk along the length of the coast path, with a specially commissioned 'razorbill' (the park's ornithological emblem) walking stick passed baton-like from community

Llidi – were at one time islands. But, fortunately for us walkers, the sea level has dropped in the intervening 70 million years.

We come around the peninsula to the bottom of Whitesands Bay, heading south now, the ground to our right seemingly disappearing seawards in shreds, leaving sudden and jagged inlets around every turn. Some of these creeks seem perfectly natural in form, with boulder-strewn beaches and barnacled caves at their bases. Others drop away suddenly and smoothly, the rock flat and precipitous, reminiscent of butter sliced by a knife, and sending even the local guillemots into fits of screams.

And then a welcome splash of colour on a day otherwise dressed in widow's weeds. The St Justinian lifeboat station is a bright red landmark on this coast. Built in 1911, it is now a listed building and, apart from launching lifeboats, is also the embarkation point for tourists wishing to see Ramsey Island, a nature reserve important for grey seals, choughs and seabirds. St Justinian itself takes its name from the sixth-century saint who lived on the island. The story goes that he was beheaded by his followers who were fed up with his strict regime. But he picked up his head and carried it over to the mainland before dying. The ruined chapel by the lifeboat station, on private land, marks his resting place. And with a view across the island like this, who can blame him?

Before you go...

Visit here

Carn Ingli
Said to be a sacred mountain, Carn Ingli rises to more than 1,100ft above sea level, with Newport Town nestling on its lower slopes. The summit offers spectacular views over the Preseli Hills – where the blue stones of Stonehenge were quarried – Nevern estuary, Newport Town, Dinas Head, Fishguard and, on a clear day, the mountain ranges of mid Wales and even a glimpse of Ireland. For the shortest, quickest route to the summit, head west from the road-side car park (grid ref SN070373)

Pentre Ifan
The most popular megalithic site in Wales, Pentre Ifan (grid ref SN099370) is a splendid burial chamber with a huge capstone poised on three uprights. Once known as Arthur's Quoit, Pentre Ifan means Ivan's Village. This monument, dating back to about 3500BC and unusually oriented north-south, stands on the slopes of a ridge commanding extensive views over the Nevern Valley.

The Old Sailors
Eat at one of Dylan Thomas' favourite seafood eateries, once known as The Sailors Safety. Head to the foreshore at Pwllgwaelod, Dinas Island, and you can't miss it.
Tel: 01348 811491

Castles
Wales is famous for its castles.
Three of the best are:

Carew
Five miles East of Pembroke, off the A477. In 1095 Gerald de Windsor received Carew Castle as part of his wife's dowry. Nothing remains of the Norman fortress. In the late 15th century Sir Rhys ap Thomas improved the castle, with the living quarters, hall and stairs built to celebrate Henry VII's new dynasty. It fell to the parliamentarians in the Civil War, but much of it still stands today.

Pembroke:
10 miles East of Milford Haven, if the A477. Sited on a mass of rock with cliffs falling to the tidal waters of the Pembroke River and Milford Haven. It was constructed between 1200 and 1210. In 1471 the Lancastrian claimant to the throne, Henry Tudor, Earl of Richmond, fled to Pembroke Castle. The Yorkists besieged the castle but Henry fled to France, returning in 1485 with 2,000 men and, at Bosworth, defeated Richard III. Henry Tudor became Henry VII. In the Civil War the castle was garrisoned by the Parliamentarians, but changed allegiance. Cromwell took the castle and slighted it so that it could not become a refuge for Royalists again. Restoration took place during the 19th century.

Manorbier's
Six miles south west of Tenby, off the B4585. Founded at the beginning of the 12th century, during the reign of Henry I, by the first Lord de Barri, and probably built as a baronial residence. The castle was never threatened and the de Barri family lived peacefully in their fortress. Today the castle is still mostly intact.

Caldey Island
A fleet of boats runs to the island from Tenby Harbour from Easter until October. Tickets can be obtained from the Caldey Island kiosk at the top of Tenby Harbour. The ticket price includes the return boat fare and landing fees. You can travel and return on any boat. Boats run every 20 minutes from 10am until about 5pm or 6pm, Monday to Friday. They also run on Saturdays from May until September between 10.30am and 4.30pm. The island is closed on Sundays, and the crossing takes about 20 minutes.

Information

Planed
The Pembrokeshire Local Action Network for Enterprise and Development has walking guides and brochures, available from tourist information centres.
Tel: 01834 860965

Tourist Information Centres
Fishguard: The Square, Fishguard
Tel: 01384 873484

St David's: The Grive, St David's
Tel: 01437 720392

Tenby: The Croft, Tenby
Tel: 01834 842404

Accommodation
Country Walking stayed with Greenways Holidays, which organises tailor-made walking breaks in the area.
Tel: 01834 862109
www.greenwaysholidays.com

Public Transport
Pembrokeshire coastal bus services
Tel: 01437 776313 or 0870 608 2608 or visit
www.pembrokeshiregreenways.co.uk

Below: Time for a spot of beachcombing before heading to St David's Head.

Left: The Blue Lagoon - once a slate quarry.

Hump-backed Wales

Offering a lair for werewolves and a sop for poets, with castles in the sky and lakes of hidden depths — the valleys and hills of the Brecon Beacons provide rich pickings for autumn walkers.

Words: **Perry Cleveland-Peck** Pictures: **Matthew Roberts**

Looking along the lumpen green spine of the Beacons, from the top of Pen y Fan.

The Fan Dance

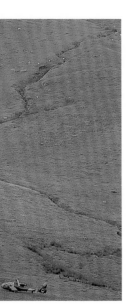

Pen y Fan is the highest peak in south Wales, and features prominently in a favourite training march of the SAS. The Fan Dance, as it is known, involves carrying a 32lb pack and a rifle over a route of about 14 miles, taking in the summits of Pen y Fan and its sister peaks, Corn Du and Cribyn. Recruits are expected to complete the yomp in four hours.

Country Walking's version of the Fan Dance consists of a leisurely bimble to the summit of Pen y Fan, via Corn Du, carrying a rucksack, waterproofs, fleece, tasty snack and water. Country Walkers are expected to complete this stroll in...well, just as long as it takes.

quite a climb. But rest assured, it's absolutely worth it.

I set out with our photographer, Matt, at about nine on a warm and humid morning. Having crossed the road from the car park, we work our way up the lower slopes of Corn Du, along the northern edge of a conifer plantation towards our high-altitude goal, the strange barking cry of a resident raven heralding our ascent. Moorland sheep break from their grazing to blink at the two-legged intruders, while the foals of Welsh ponies stare out at us from beneath mother's scraggy mane.

> "The air here seems to have been piped in from Heaven itself."

The SAS Fan Dance and the Country Walking Fan Dance start at the same place – the Storey Arms mountain rescue centre on the A470. Here the similarities end. But don't get me wrong. Our Fan Dance is by no means for the faint hearted. At 2,906ft above sea level, the summit of Pen y Fan is

Underfoot, the path is well established. Blocks of red sandstone have been set into the ground almost all the way to the summit and provide a fine surface for boots to grip during the steep bits – it's an excellent path. Indeed, as Matt and I hit the summit of Corn Du, thinking for all the world that

Above: A weary Perry – Country Walking's very own version of the SAS

we are Mallory and Irving, we spot a path-building party working on the high slopes of Pen y Fan, a few hundred metres to the north east. These conscientious and diligent workers climb to the top of Pen y Fan every day before they even think about starting the back-breaking work of constructing paths. And then, after a day of this, they walk back down again. Quite amazing, and something that puts our humble efforts into perspective.

Nevertheless, it is with a real sense of achievement that I survey the views from the top of Pen y Fan.

The great hills and valleys form folds and ridges in the earth that seem like giant sleeping beasts. Occasional clouds slip by beneath us, at once hiding and revealing a lake in the valley below. The air here seems to have been piped in from Heaven itself.

You need to take your time when walking these high routes. Pace yourself. And if it's warm, packing some insect repellent is advised – the midges have a ferocious appetite. But after the bites have stopped itching, it will be the memory of this special place and the satisfaction of having got there that will stay with you – forever!

The Route

Distance: *8km/5 miles.*
Start: *Park at the Storey Arms Mountain Rescue Centre on the A470 (grid ref SO983204). Cross the road and take a track north east alongside a plantation. Climb to Corn Du and then Pen y Fan. Take a track south west around Corn Du summit and, eventually, along the southern edge of a plantation. Head up the road back to the car park.*
Maps: *Ordnance Survey Outdoor Leisure 12, Harvey Superwalker Brecon Beacons East.*
For more information: *Call the Storey Arms on 01874 623598.*

Aquatic drama

The perfect antidote to Pen y Fan is a stroll along the banks of the Mellte River and its series of stunning waterfalls. If the mountains offer huge, open, solitary spaces, this waterfall walk is rammed with so much breathtaking flora, fauna and geology that it seems all of nature has been condensed into one six-mile hike.

To treat myself I begin at Porth yr Ogof, where the Mellte disappears underground through the yawning mouth of the Porth yr Ogof caves. The cave mouth, located at the bottom of a deep limestone gorge, is the largest cave entrance in Wales.

> "I get my first glimpse of these mighty cascades. The Mellte crashes down a series of limestone steps. Can it get better than this? Well yes, actually."

As I descend from the car park, the temperature drops suddenly and noticeably, the cool Mellte waters and shady limestone rocks providing the best natural air conditioning that I have ever come across.

Lush, verdant trees and ferns bedeck the steep gorge sides, and ivy creepers hang from rocks above the cave entrance like the forelocks of some fossilised dragon. What a perfect place to cool off before the walk downstream.

The path to the falls is over a road that runs across the top of the caves. To walk it is to step into some enchanted place – the likes of which even Tolkien's hobbits would find bewitching. Gnarly roots of ancient oaks and ashes twist from between mossy boulders and limestone rocks, criss-crossing the muddy path. The sound of water, whispering and murmuring its way south, serves as a constant and alluring soundtrack to the journey – and a teasing hint of our goal.

Occasionally, the leafy canopy parts to reveal wildflower meadows, thick with buttercups, saxifrage and grasses. A rare dipper skims the river's surface, weaving between submerged rocks that look like the heads of wallowing hippopotamuses.

As the Mellte's roar becomes louder, my pace quickens with anticipation. Water vapour thickens the air and the blood in my veins seems to surge, in tune with the great Mellte itself.

Turning around a corner and edging beneath a hanging rock, I get my first glimpse of these mighty cascades. The Mellte crashes down Sgwd Clun-Gwyn (Waterfall of the White Thigh), a series of great limestone steps carved, it seems, for some ancient Celtic leviathan. Can it get better than this?

Well yes, actually. There are another four of these waterfalls on this river. My favourite is Sgwd Isaf Clun-Gwyn, which with its curved shape suggests a watery amphitheatre.

The landscape here certainly provides enough drama for its stage. Question is, what will it do for an encore?

The Route

Distance: *9.7km/6 miles.*
Start: *Follow steps to the caves from a car park near Cwm Porth (grid ref SO928125). The start of the waterfalls path is across the road, opposite the car park entrance. Head south for the waterfalls, enjoy, then head north back along the river or through the forest to the car park.*
Maps: *Ordnance Survey Outdoor Leisure 12, Harvey Superwalker Brecon Beacons West. A map of circular and linear routes around the valley is available at the car park.*

Top: The yawning cave at Porth yr Ogof
Bottom: The rare dipper that Perry raves about?

Sgwd Isaf Clun-Gwyn. Gorge-ous!

Welsh 'rarebit'

I love castles. All those knights and damsels in distress and stuff. It brings out the Robin Hood in me. Wales has more than its fair share of castles. It seems to have one on every other hillside. In fact, sheep and castles are my defining memories of the Beacons. Oh, and rain. Sheep, castles and rain – love it.

But if there's one castle every walker worth his boots should see it's that of Carreg Cennen on the western edge of the park. This is no ruin of a few stones and an ice cream van. This doesn't require mind-bending feats of imagination to envisage

> **"The castle sits on top of a hill about 900ft above sea level. The views are staggering."**

what it must have been like. Carreg Cennen is a full-blown, living and breathing fortification that looks as if it could survive an all-out attack by any of today's elite forces. Some 800 years after it was built, Carreg Cennen remains a castle with attitude.

Not to say altitude. The castle sits on top of a hill about 900ft above sea level. The views are staggering. On one side, a sheer 300ft cliff protects the site from marauding interlopers. And hidden in the countryside around the castle are many historical and natural features, from the underground source of the River Loughor, to early 20th-century limekilns, Bronze Age burial sites known as pillow mounds and shake holes where underground caves have collapsed.

So don't give in to temptation and march straight to the drawbridge. Be strong. Park at the castle car park and take the circular walk that descends in the Cennen valley and through the castle woodlands. It's a four-and-a-half-mile waymarked route and you can go either way around. Think of it as working up an appetite for the great feast itself – leaving the consummate Welsh rarebit on your plate until last!

Thirsty work

"But it's just a single rock," says Matt. "Why bother with it?" Why bother indeed? It's a good question. And one I'm unsure how to answer. Why invest so much time and energy – physical and mechanical – to visit a single stone?

But on our arrival at Maen Llia (grid ref SO923193), which stands upright and alone beneath the mountains of Fan Llia to the east and Fann Nedd to the west, above the river valley of Afon Llia, it all just seems to make sense. After all, the people who erected it so many years ago spent quite a bit of time and energy doing so, and some believe that Maen Llia has an energy all of its own. Who knows?

Folklore suggests that when the mood takes it, Maen Llia gets up and takes a stroll to the nearest stream to quench its thirst. And how many of us walkers can say that we don't enjoy a walk with a drink at its end? Perhaps that's why I have to see this standing stone. It is a living legend after my own heart.

The heol

In 1875, Spanish opera diva Adelina Patti set up home in Craig-y-nos. The Britney Spears of her day, Patti was extremely wealthy and had fans all over the world. She was even said to be a 'great friend' of Edward VII.

She built a castle at Craig-y-nos to entertain her society friends. But why here, at this remote spot? Local people like to think it was because of the 'heol' – the love of the Welsh valleys. And who can blame her?

The castle is now a walkers' hostel extraordinaire. Food and drink, not to mention a little live jazz, can be enjoyed at the castle's three bars, and, if you're lucky, you might even be able to take in an opera recital.

There are numerous walks from Craig-y-nos, but my favourite is the 'Legendary Ladies Walk'. It links Craig-y-nos and Llan y Fan Fawr, taking in the haunting Cerrig Duon stone circle and Maen Mawr standing stone – an ideal spot for lunch.

Find out more: To book beds and visit events at Craig-y-nos Castle, call 01639 730205.

Dylan dally

Dylan Thomas is still massively influential, and books on the great man continue to be published. One recent tome, The Dylan Thomas Trail, by David N Thomas, is a collection of walks around key places in Dylan's life.

Before I left for Wales, I spoke to the author, who told me of a Dylan Thomas walk over Black Mountain that doesn't feature in his book. It does, however, feature a most fortifying conclusion.

"Two of Dylan's favourite drinking holes were The Plough in Glanaman, and the Cennen Arms in Trapp – either side of Black Mountain," says David. "Dylan was an obsessive walker, and it was while walking that he composed his poems."

Sadly, The Plough in Glanaman no longer exists. But it is with great (hiccup) pleasure that I can inform you the Cennen Arms is still there. Its surrounding countryside is indeed inspirational. And after a stroll across the moors and couple of pints of local bitter, you, too, will be talking in verse.

Lady of the lake

Llyn y Fan Fawr is an enchanted place. A glacial lake, it is about half a kilometre long and half again as wide, and the best part of 2,000ft above sea level. It lies at the foot of the imposing Fan Brycheiniog cliffs. Fan Fawr and its sister lake Llyn y Fan Fach, a short way due west, ooze folklore and tales of mysterious goings-on.

So it seems appropriate that the elements have conspired to cobble together some serious Welsh rain, which comes at me through fickle mists and low cloud. This is definitely going to be one of those map-and-compass walks. I'm just thankful that I remembered to pack my GPS unit.

So, having fixed the position of the car and taken a bearing, I set out for the lake. A track is clearly visible on the map, though in reality I find it hard to pick out in the mist. It crosses a number of small brooks, water hissing and bubbling down occasional craggy cascades, and picks its way through springy heather towards the cliffs. The heady smell of sheep and peat pervades the damp air. As I approach the lake, the ground becomes wetter; reeds and thick mosses sprout from the marshy earth, like tufts of unkempt hair on an early-morning hillwalker.

With visibility reduced I am just able to make out the brooding Fan Brycheiniog cliffs, but unable to judge the distance to the lake. Each time I top a rise in the moorland, another one tantalisingly rolls out ahead. But I persevere through the gloom, and come upon the lake suddenly, mists parting like curtains to reveal the body of water.

For many years the people of Brecon made an annual pilgrimage to Fan Fawr. Legend has it that on the first Sunday in August, a water nymph with the torso and head of a beautiful woman and the lower half of a dolphin would rise from boiling waters, and comb her hair in the reflection of the water. Will the lady of the lake show herself today?

The Route

Distance: *9.8km/6 miles.*
Start: *You can park in a lay-by (grid ref SO856223). Follow a track west south west to Llyn y Fan Fawr. From the lake, follow the Nant y Llyn stream to Maen Mawr and Cerrig Duon stone circle (grid ref SO852206). Head north up the River Tawe and then follow the road back to the lay-by.*
Maps: *Ordnance Survey Outdoor Leisure 12, Harvey Superwalker Brecon Beacons West.*

> "This is an enchanted place. Llyn y Fan Fawr and its sister lake Llyn y Fan Fach, a short way due west, ooze folklore and tales of mysterious goings-on."

Walk a Roman road

Ever wondered why Roman roads are straight? It's so the emperors' wives could get to the shops quickly. Or so it would appear, if the story behind Sarn Helen has any truth to it.

A medieval Welsh tale tells of how a Roman emperor, Macsen Wledig (thought to be the real life Magnus Maximus, emperor in 383), fell in love with and married a beautiful Welsh woman called Elen Luydogg, after dreaming about her. Part of her wedding gift was the construction of three castles. But Elen – or Helen – wasn't happy about all the off-road riding to and from her country piles, and demanded some highways. Sarn Helen (Helen's Road) is one of them, and some of it is still there today.

> "Wonder why Roman roads are straight? It's so emperors' wives could get to the shops quickly."

When, some 2,000 years later, I cross the River Nedd on my journey along the same road, it soon becomes clear that this is no ordinary track. This one has been around for a while. Parts of the exposed stone slabs are still visible under my feet, structured and regular like the legions of troops that must have built it.

This is a delightfully airy walk. It's well-defined throughout and reasonably level, which makes it ideal for a stroll with all the family. And if the empty moorlands prove a little monotonous, you can nip off the track and visit the potholes at Pwll-y-rhyd. But I'm eager to get to the Maen Madoc standing stone, which lies beside Sarn Helen at the crest of the final hill. It's a slender, nine-foot monument of Celtic origin. Interestingly, it has some Roman graffiti written on it in Latin. Translated it reads, "Dervacus, son of Justus. He lies here." Sensible lad.

The Route

Distance: 10km/61/4 miles.
Start: Start at Ystradfellte car park. Head west at the crossroads and pick up the footpath to Pwll-y-rhyd caves. Explore the caves if you like. Cross the River Nedd north of the caves and pick up Sarn Helen. Head north, going over the River Nedd again.
Pass Maen Mawr (grid ref SO918158) and go through a plantation to the road. Head south back to Ystradfellte.
Maps: Ordnance Survey Outdoor Leisure 12, Harvey Superwalker Brecon Beacons West.

Beastly behaviour

Few people know of it, but there's a spot just north of the national park, by Abergwesyn Common, to be exact, that is notorious for beasts of the night. Yes, where dark and fearful creatures dwell. But do you have the nerve to walk with werewolves?

Well, not real werewolves, actually. But the next best thing. Abergwesyn was the location for the werewolf attack scene at the beginning of the horror film, An American Werewolf in London – you know the bit, where the two young men have just left the Slaughtered Lamb pub having been advised to "Stay on the roads. Keep clear of the moors," and, "Beware the Moon, lads," only to immediately walk off the road and get munched by a man wearing a prosthetic face. Marvellous stuff.

You can see why the director chose this spot. Solitary houses lie at the base of steep valley sides, furnished with swathes of trees. Crystal streams and rivers bubble along valley floors, often to vast reservoirs such as Llyn Brianne. The presence of the old phonebox that features in the film lends the area a surreal air.

This, sadly, is the last walk of my Brecons trip and the evening is well upon us when Matt, Country Walking's photographer, and I park up. The air is thick with earthy aromas and seems to rejuvenate us with every breath.

As the rain comes down, and I tug on my waterproofs, the infamous line, "Beware the Moon, lads," echoes around my head. To keep our spirits up, Matt and I head to a viewpoint west of the phonebox, above Llyn Berwyn.

As we walk I notice that, somehow, we've stepped off the road and on to open moorland. Matt seems strangely silent, his facial hair suddenly more noticeable in the half-light. I ask if he feels all right, and comment on how big his teeth look, when, with a rabid stare and a wolf-like howl, he bounds across the hills. "Yeah, yeah, stop mucking about, Matt. It isn't funny. Matt, Matt…"

The Route

Distance: *13km/8 miles.*
Start: *Park at Cwm Berwyn plantation (grid ref SN738575). Head north across Esgair Fawr, to a path that runs west-east. Head east to a standing stone. Head south to the phonebox (grid ref SN763576). Follow the road west back to the car park.*
Maps: *Ordnance Survey Explorer 187.*

Secrets of Snowdonia

We find local experts to guide you on the best routes to the finest views in north Wales.

Words: **Perry Cleveland-Peck and Julian Rollins** Pictures: **Tom Bailey and Neil Hepworth**

The Hollywood actor Anthony Hopkins, famed for his portrayal of the deliciously evil screen baddie Hannibal Lecter in Silence Of The Lambs, recently donated £1 million pounds to a Welsh mountain. Not just any mountain, mind, but the mountain from which much of North Wales takes its name – Snowdon.

Believe it or not, Hopkins's Hannibal, yes him of the "fava beans and a nice chianti", and us walkers have something in common. No, we're not talking cannibalism. We're talking about a fascination for secrets. Hannibal, no doubt, has one or two of his own. But he also flirts with, torments and finally helps the FBI during its investigation into someone else's darker secrets.

We walkers also like to flirt with secrets, be they of a less blood-thirsty and more bucolic nature. Indeed, tell a walker of a secret view, a little-known historic twist to a trail or a recently discovered snicket, and he'll be pulling on his gaiters quicker than Jodie Foster can shout, "Who turned the lights out?".

With this in mind, we at Country Walking have revisited the area so beloved of Mr Hopkins to investigate the routes known only to the locals, the holders-of-the-secrets. So whether it is Cadair Idris in the company of a national park warden, long-lost paths alongside a resident archaeologist, undiscovered routes through the slate mines of yesteryear, or the trails that the Everest team trained on, prepare yourself for some secrets of Snowdonia. All is about to be revealed.

Cadair Idris

A giant of a mountain, with more than a little fizz

Above: Myfyr and Perry begin their ascent, beside an alternative spelling sign.

Myfyr Tomos is a Snowdonia National Park warden. He has lived in and around Snowdonia all his life, walking the many and diverse trails this area has to offer since he first put one foot in front of the other.

So you'd think that, what with all the guided walks, footpath surveys and occasional rescues he is obliged to do, Myfyr would look further afield for his own walking pleasure – Scotland, perhaps, or the Lakes. Think again, for there is one Snowdonia landscape to which Myfyr returns again and again, and that is Cadair Idris.

Cadair Idris is an isolated lump in the south of Snowdonia. In fact, Cadair Idris is a range of four summits, Penygadair being the highest at 2,929ft. Like the mountain that lends its name to the entire national park, Cadair Idris is actually the title of the massif, not the summit. No matter, the walk to the top offers some truly spectacular views and impressive crags, home to playful peregrines, wheatear and stonechats.

Also like Snowdon, Cadair Idris has a history of refreshments being served up on its summit, though, despite the presence of the stone shelter where they were once served, this doesn't occur today. And like Snowdon, Cadair is associated with a giant – the mythical creature Idris. Alternatively, the mountain is also said to take its name from a warrior killed in battle against the Saxons in about 630AD, though there is some confusion about the exact history.

> "Suddenly Llyn Cau stretches about before us, a magical pool of water some 400 metres wide, clear as glass and bone-chillingly cold, despite today's warm conditions."

"I'm not entirely sure about the mountain and its name," says Myfyr stepping out ahead of us, "but I know that the Idris ginger beer company takes its name from the mountain."

Myfyr, photographer Tom and I are setting off from the Minffordd side of the mountain to the south, a carpet of fading bluebells seemingly rolled out for us, inviting us to the woods ahead. Close to the visitor centre, Myfyr points out a derelict, roofless stone building. "That used to be a lemonade factory," he says. We peer inside a glass window, voracious ivy tugging at some ancient drink-production machinery, hauntingly echoing an era gone by.

We pick up the Minffordd path and head north up a series of steps through a broadleaf wood. The steps are steep – this is the toughest stretch of our entire walk – but the oak and elm canopy keeps us cool in the sunlight, while the sheets of water that tumble over the rocky cascades of Nant Cadair to our right lend a refreshing song to the air. The broadleaf trees turn to conifers before, with one final push, the views open out for a wide grassy pasture, the remains of several hafod – or shepherds' summer dwellings – scattered hither and yon.

Myfyr points out a number of fenced enclosures, areas that the Countryside Council for Wales are keeping from the sheep in order to ascertain the effects of grazing on the hillside. Willow and rowan trees grow behind the fences, proof that the flanks of Cadair would look entirely different were it not for the ubiquitous nonchalant sheep.

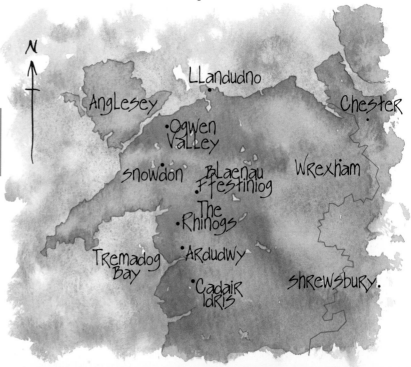

We head on past the enclosures, the anticipation of the lake that sits beneath the Cadair horseshoe ever growing as we breast each of the subtle rises that keep it hidden from view. Then suddenly Llyn Cau stretches out before us, a magical pool some 400m wide, clear as glass and bone-chillingly cold, despite today's warm conditions.

"It's about 60m deep," says Myfyr. "We sent some divers down there recently. At the bottom there is a vast standing stone, a great finger of rock that, I guess, fell off the mountain and embedded itself."

I consider this for a while, and decide that a more likely cause for this secret menhir is the giant Idris, who put it there in a moment of Goliath-like mischief.

After a brief sip from the flask we head south up to Craig Lwyd and then west for our first summit, Craig Cwm Amarch. The ground is loose beneath our feet and, for a brief moment, I'm jealous of Myfyr's walking poles. But the spectacular views over Tal-y-llyn lake, with the sea winking in the distance, more than make up for it.

Then its on to Craig Cau, pleated and crinkled, with sheer drops to the water below in every rocky fold. We lose a few hundred metres with a descent to the Bwlch Cau col, the granite around us turning to mud stone as we cross some ancient seam. Then it's the final push for the top, strange pillow lava formations indicating that our high-altitude goal was once very much underwater.

But there is nothing bottom-dwelling about our new situation. We reach the top of Penygadair and take a good look around. Myfyr points out Snowdon on the horizon, and the lake of Llyn y Gadair beneath the northern face of Cadair. A skylark plays on the updrafts below us. Everything seems right in the world.

"It's a forgiving mountain," says Myfyr. "Things do go wrong, but on the whole it is a matter of people being inconvenienced rather than lost. Cadair Idris is a very friendly mountain."

And with that, we head for home.

The Route

Cadair Idris

Distance: *9.7km/6 miles.*
Time: 5 hours.
Terrain: *Steep woodland, grassy hillsides, rocky summit with some scree.*
Route: *From Minffordd car park (grid ref SH732116) head north west to Dol-y-cae. Pick up footpath heading west to Llyn Cau. Head south to Craig Llwyd, then west along ridge to Craig Cau, then on to Penygadair. For the fourth summit, pick up the Pony Path to Cyfrwy (grid ref SH704133). From Penygadair follow ridge to Mynydd Moel. At the north-south fence, pick up path (not on some maps) heading south to woods. Cross stream and return via earlier woodland path.*
Map: *Ordnance Survey Explorer OL23.*

The Rhinogs
A magical nature reserve with a capricious character

"Did you see the goats?" It is almost the first thing that Jonathan Neale, who works with the Countryside Council for Wales, asks us on meeting up.

"They were on the road, just a little way back. I was sure you would have stopped to get a picture."

Well, no we hadn't. The Rhinog nature reserve is one of Wales' best, and a great place to see Snowdonia's wildlife oddity – wild goats. These elusive renegades have been holed up here for a

"Our walk takes us up to the flank of Rhinog Fawr, along time-tested footings, the Roman Steps, great slabs of stone worn smooth by countless feet down the centuries."

The Route

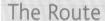

Rhinog Nature Reserve
Distance: 12km/7 1/2 miles.
Time: 3 hours.
Terrain: Very rocky, rugged going.
Route: From car park at Cwm Bychan (grid ref SH647315) take the path south and climb Roman Steps. Follow ridge path north to meet path along banks of Afon Crawcwellt (grid ref SH682332). This path drops down to the Cwm Bychan road close to the car park. For further details about walking in the Rhinog reserve call 01248 372333.
Map: Ordnance Survey Explorer OL18.

century or more, since escaping farmyard captivity. We'd been hoping for a glimpse of the outlaws, but a photo would have been better.

"We'll probably see some more later," says Jonathan, as we set off in the opposite direction. Centuries back most farms would have kept a few goats, Jonathan informs us, their job being to graze in the most inaccessible spots, so the more valuable sheep and cattle would not be tempted to take risks.

In a way, the goats have the credentials to recommend the best Snowdonia routes – avoiding human contact as far as possible, the goats keep to the wildest, most out-of-the-way corners of Snowdonia.

As it turns out, we don't see hide nor hair of a wild goat for the rest of our walk. They may be here, but walking the Rhinogs doesn't offer much in the way of horizon-scanning opportunities. You watch your feet too closely for that.

That said, having a scientist along for the day turns out to be useful. When you turn an ankle it hurts just the same, but at least you can discover exactly what type of rock is the offender.

In this case it is an especially resilient Cambrian gritstone that seems to have it in for walkers. It makes for slow, careful progress, that allows only an occasional glance at the scenery. But when you do chance it, the views are hard to beat.

That said, the first section of our walk takes us up to the flank of Rhinog Fawr along time-tested

footings, the Roman Steps, great slabs of stone worn smooth by countless feet down the centuries. They probably aren't Roman, although they did build the arrow-straight road a few miles to the east. Jonathan says it is probably a medieval packhorse route.

It is only at the top of the steps, up above the last stunted, wind-battered tree, that we see the sea. It looks close. As the crow flies – or the goat bounds – Cwm Bychan, with its ring of rock around a peaceful lake, is only about four miles from the coast road and 'civilisation'. But the road that delivers you to the parking field at the end of Llyn Cwm Bychan is so convoluted that it seems to take forever to get there.

Stopping for lunch, we look east across the dense forest of Coed y Brenin and do some peak spotting. Soaking up the silence, Jonathan expands on why the Rhinog reserve is his favourite.

"I don't get the time to go walking that often these days. But when I do, I come here. It is a special place with a magic all of its own."

The magic is, he says, all about the space and the peace of the place, as well as the fact that it is a wilderness that man has largely failed to tame. Just like the goats, in fact.

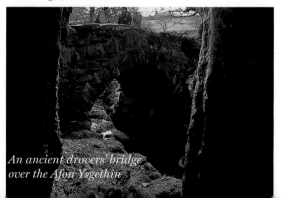
An ancient drovers' bridge over the Afon Ysgethin

Ardudwy

Ancient tracks and artefacts – just step this way

Andrew Weir talks and drives with equal amounts of enthusiasm. He is a lecturer at the national park education centre, and his course on Snowdonia's ancient tracks and pathways involves a lot of walking. His favourite route – the one we are off to find – goes through countryside that has become his classroom.

"This is a multi-layered landscape," he says, pausing briefly to shift down a gear. "Generations have left their mark here, putting layer after layer of history on what you see around you."

Ahead is a broad sweep of hills, where the southern tail of the Rhinogs coils down to the sea at Barmouth. You can see for miles, and there is lots to see – sheep, rocks, gorse and stone walls, but no people. Today the place is our own.

Until recently, Ardudwy, this now overlooked corner of north Wales, was full of people. Andrew says, "This area was a relatively comfortable place to live, and I think people did pretty well. But they were cut off from the world beyond. When they travelled they had to do it by foot. That meant going over the Rhinogs, taking the line of least resistance."

We start out along one of those routes, a path that finds its way eventually to the town of Dolgellau through a pass in the hills called the Gap of the Drovers – Bwlch y Rhiwgyr. The drovers were, of course, the cowboys of Wales' west, who drove cattle east to the markets of England in the days before railways.

As antiques go, this path does not at first look that convincing – it has a metalled top. But along the line of the old path, says Andrew, you can find clues that prove that people have been passing through here for thousands of years.

To prove the point, in just a short uphill stretch of walking he points out a neolithic stone tomb and evidence of a long-lost Bronze Age settlement. Just away from the path, in a dip by a wall, a ring of earth marks a medieval barn or house, or a mixture of both.

Altogether they show that people have been coming and going this way for a very long time, and throughout our walk Andrew has stories to match just about every landmark we pass. Almost home, we pause and he says, "For me, what is so good about walking here is that you are walking in the footsteps of people who have gone before you long ago."

The Route

Ancient tracks
Distance: *12.5km/7 3/4 miles.*
Time: *3 1/2 hours.*
Terrain: Long climbs, but paths good.
Route: *From grid ref SH602231 take track south, crossing Afon Ysgethin. Keep right (south east) to Bwlch y Rhiwgyr pass. After the pass, follow ridge north to drop down to the bridge over the Ysgethin at Pont-Scethin (grid ref SH635235). Where path meets a track, turn left and head back to the start. For details of courses at Plas Tan y Bwlch call 01766 590324.*
Map: *Ordnance Survey Explorer OL18.*

A burial chamber near the start – just one of this area's many links with the past.

Blaenau FFestiniog

Don't slate this hidden treasure

In a bookshop I'd had a quick scan through a guidebook. It didn't pull its punches. Blaenau Ffestiniog was, it told me, ugly and best avoided. Indeed, the people who drew up the boundaries of the national park half a century ago seem to have shared that opinion, putting a big ring around the town that excludes it from the park.

Ugly seems a bit harsh, but the town's past as the centre of Snowdonia's slate mining industry has certainly left its mark. Hugged in by mountains and huge heaps of slate spoil, Blaenau Ffestiniog does have a reputation that keeps some people away.

Which makes Denis McAteer's choice for a walk seem a little unusual. Denis is chairman of The Ramblers' Association in north Wales. We meet outside Blaenau's cottage hospital, tucked between tight streets of terraced houses. Our route heads out of town to the south, and things do not look too promising. Surely this is the local teenagers' hang-out, and not one of Snowdonia's best-kept secrets?

The view though, when it arrives, is a classic; for hospital patients it must be the finest tonic. From our position under the Moelwyns, the whole of southern Snowdonia is set out in front of us, and we head in its direction.

Down the valley, away from the town, Denis starts selling us the joys of Blaenau Ffestiniog. As we take a break to study the tumbling water of the Afon Goedol, he explains that he often brings walkers here in the hope of winning them over. "People are surprised at how good it is. I think they expect little, so when they give this place a chance they get very enthusiastic about it."

We work our way on through the ancient oak woodland of Coed Cymerau, where the tree trunks look as though they've been lagged against the cold with a thick blanket of spongy green moss. And, as we walk, Denis finally gets around to revealing why he has such a personal loyalty to Blaenau Ffestiniog – it's his home town.

"I've known this place for as long as I can remember, so I suppose it is special to me," he says. "The town has its problems, and I'd like to see it as part of the national park, so it could get a share of the benefits that come through attracting visitors."

Which seems fair, because Blaenau Ffestiniog has had a tough time of it. As you walk, the area's blue-gray slate is everywhere – this is its history. Slate once covered the roofs of Victorian Britain and much of the rest of world, and at the turn of the 20th century the local slate mines and quarries were producing half a million tons a year.

But despite a mini-boom after the Second World War, the slate industry eventually slumped into terminal decline, the mines closing in the 1950s.

Through woods overhanging the crystal-clear falls and deep pools of Afon Teigl, we begin our climb back towards the town, visible in the distance on its shelf at the head of its valley. At one point a collection of ruined cottages stand just off the path, and we make a detour for a closer look.

The roofless remains of the cottages look as though they've been abandoned for 1,000 years. But garden shrubs grown to giant size suggest that the house-holders are not that long gone.

As we head past the first houses on the outskirts of town, Denis passes the time of day with a local, the first person we've seen for miles. And that, says Denis, is one of the beauties of Blaenau.

"I can be here in the middle of summer and walk this route and not meet anybody. That can't be bad, can it?"

The Route

Blaenau Ffestiniog
Distance: *9km/5 1/2 miles.*
Time: *2 1/2 miles.*
Terrain: *Good paths, some steep climbs.*
Route: *Park close to hospital (grid ref SH702456). From hill on right of hospital, take path which follows Afon Bowydd to A496. Turn right. After 50m cross to path over bridge. Soon after take path along Afon Goedol. At stone bridge cross into woods and follow path to reach Rhyd-y-sarn. Cross A496 and go right. After 100m take track on left to circle around to cross Afon Teigl. Keep to northern bank as far as minor road. Turn left, then go over stone stile near road junction. Cross field to gate on to road, then take path opposite to stone steps over a wall. Take path down to A496, but do not go on to road. Instead, turn right, passing ruined house. At railway line do not cross the bridge, but turn left to climb back to hospital.*
Map: *Ordnance Survey Explorer OL18.*

Snowdon

If there is one walk you should do in Wales, it is Snowdon. Not only because Snowdon is the mountain from which this entire national park takes its name. Not only because its (in)famous summit café is about to disappear. And not only because Snowdon is, quite simply, a fantastic high-altitude place to walk.

But mainly because it is on this mountain that both George Mallory and Andrew Irvine, and Sir

> "We round a corner and above us, on the horizon, we spot the marker stone at Bwlch Glas, a gnarled rocky finger that points heavenwards in perpetuity, somehow poignant in its vast loneliness."

Edmund Hillary, came to train before their respective expeditions to Mount Everest – Sir Edmund's resulting in the first successful ascent of Everest.

Now we here at Country Walking are not suggesting in any way that you should walk Snowdon in practice for climbing Everest. Heavens, most of us have enough trouble climbing out of bed in the morning! All we're saying is that if there is a time and a place to do something, and if that something just happens to be a wink and a nod to one of the greatest human achievements, then a saunter on Snowdon is surely one way to do it.

That, at least, is how I see it, though as I glance over at Tom, Country Walking's usually-amiable photographer, who seems to be staring out of the windscreen at some non-object in the middle distance, I'm not entirely sure I'm in the majority.

"Come on, Tom," I say. "Quarter-to-six is a perfectly reasonable time to start walking up a mountain."

Tom must still be half asleep – dreaming of dogs, apparently, because he simply growls in reply.

There are a number of routes to Snowdon's summit. You can try the Llanberis Path, which hugs the railway line that runs from the village of Llanberis south to Snowdon's top. You can try the Miners' Track, originally an access path to mines on

Top: The stone finger at Bwlch Glas

Above: The summit of Snowdon

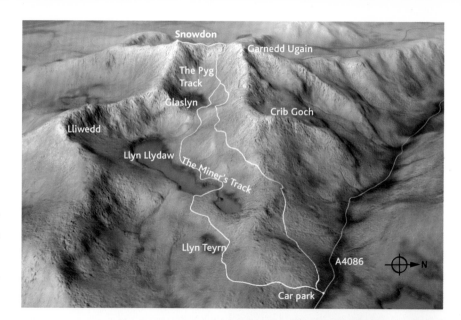

the eastern side of the mountain. Or you can attempt the southerly Watkin Path, where our Everest heroes trained for their little jolly in the Himalayas – though we wouldn't recommend it to anyone less than experienced.

Tom and I opt for the Pyg Track, for a number of reasons. It's a walkable yet exhilarating route to the top; one that skirts the southern slopes of Snowdon's sister, the mighty Crib Goch; and one that takes in the mystical and enchanting waters of Llyn Llydaw and Glaslyn, which we'll experience from a beguiling eagle-eye vantage point high above them. But mainly because it starts halfway up the mountain.

To be honest, daybreak is probably the best time to commence business on Snowdon. The mountain pulls in walkers from the world over, and if you don't start out early you may as well turn around and head for the Bluewater retail park – the escalators there will probably be less congested. Even with an early start, you'll start running into people on your way back down to base camp, but the look on their faces is worth the intrusion.

Like the Minffordd path on Cadair, the Pyg Track starts off steeply but soon evens out to a steady, friendly climb. This morning, with the early morning mist still hanging in the valleys below and the blood-orange, watercolour sunrise lighting our hearts as well as our way, it seems as if we are the only people on this strangely cratered planet, though the occasional teasing, haunting screeches of the resident ravens echo off the mountain sides, a cross between a baby's cry and an angle-grinder.

We round a corner and above us, on the horizon, we spot the marker stone at Bwlch Glas, a gnarled rocky finger that points heavenwards in perpetuity, somehow poignant in its vast loneliness.

The last zig-zag push to the top is tough, make no bones about it, but it's thankfully short, and soon we arrive at Bwlch Glas just beneath Snowdon's summit. After such a climb it's hard to adjust to the sight of the railway line, like swimming alone for hours across the Channel straight into a busy lido, but we push on for the café and the trig point at the top, the whole world spreading out beneath us. It's only 8.30am. I rummage for the mobile – now who can I get out of bed?

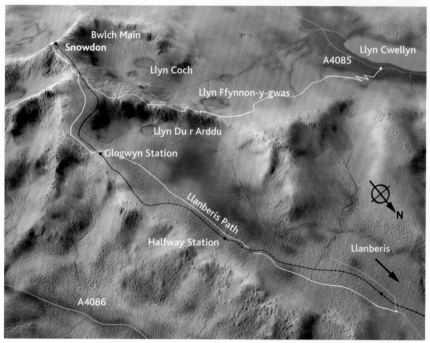

The Route

The Pyg Track
Distance: *10.5km/6½ miles.*
Time: *3-4 hours.*
Terrain: *Rocky slopes, some steep, stepped climbs.*
Route: *From Pen-y-pass (grid ref SH647557) head west above Llyn Llydaw to Bwlch y Moch. Continue west above the Glaslyn lake before zig-zagging to the finger stone at Bwlch Glas. Head south to Snowdon. Return via the same route.*
Map: *Ordnance Survey Explorer OL17.*

Ogwen valley
A fascinating corner of Snowdonia with views of Anglesey

Above: Slate fencing echoes the industry of yesteryear

Our starting point is just outside Penrhyn Castle in Llandygai, a village built to house the servants who once worked at the castle. We are, says Margaret Fernley, within the castle's huge outer wall, although we can't see it.

Maybe it's because I'm parched, but I have some sympathy for the people of Llandygai. When Lord Penrhyn gave them a village of new homes, it was on the condition that it never had the corrupting influence of a pub.

Llandygai and its castle are in a fascinating corner of Snowdonia. The Carneddau mountains are a powerful backdrop, a vast area of upland that drops rather sharply to meet the sea.

Margaret, her husband Neville, photographer Neil and I get under way, walking past Llandygai's pretty cottages and church. Recent changes have rather downplayed Lord Penrhyn's dominance. The new A55 is now the biggest thing around. It cuts across the countryside just a stone's throw from the castle, and our route takes us under the road as it hops the Afon Ogwen.

But the traffic noise is quickly masked by the gentler roar of the river, and we are soon much closer to the past than to today. Margaret is a great enthusiast for this history. She was born not far from Llandygai. And as a stalwart of the local Ramblers' Association, she has the opportunity to share her passion with a now thriving local group that attracts as many as 40 people on its walks.

As we cross a narrow footbridge over the Ogwen, Neville points out the ubiquitous slate fencing. This, too, is mining country. Like gappy teeth, the strips of slate stand out of the ground in rows, linked together by strands of wire. They are, says Neville, much in demand these days, and so tend to disappear into the backs of vans on dark nights.

We move up and out of the valley and take a detour to look at one of the oldest houses in the

Below: Llandygai church, where castle servants once prayed

area, Cochwillan. It is an old hall, thought to have been built by a former sheriff of Caernarvonshire, who was lucky enough to back the winning side at the Battle of Bosworth in 1485. These days you have to make an appointment to visit the grounds.

We are blessed with a blue sky day, and looking west we are rewarded with fantastic views over the sea and the flat land Anglesey. This really is great walking country, and that is how Margaret, a fierce defender of walkers' rights, intends to keep it.

She tells us of her own battle – one to keep a single path from disappearing, which became a major story in Wales.

"People used the paths to get to work and to get to school," she says. "They were part of their lives. If we let any of that go without a fight, we are letting those people down."

I'll drink to that.

Below: Wandering beside the Ogwen River near Halfway Bridge

Before you go...

Left: The Aber Falls - one of Wales' finest waterfalls with great views across the Menai Straits

Stay here

Pen-y-Gwyrd, close to Snowdon

An Everest homage in Snowdonia is not complete without a stay at the Pen-y-Gwyrd Hotel. It was here that the heroes of 1953 stayed while training in Snowdonia. The hotel is about a mile east of Pen-y-pass on the junction of the A4086 and the A498. It has 16 rooms, a lounge, a bar that serves food, plus a sauna and swimming pool. For more information call 01286 870221 or visit www.pyg.co.uk

The Courthouse, Betws-y-Coed

This walker-friendly B&B once served as the town's police station. Each of the 10 rooms has a judicial theme, and all have en-suite bathroom facilities, apart from the Prison Cell room. Hearty breakfast fare is provided with bacon and sausages sourced from local producers. Guests have full use of the lounge and riverside garden. For more details call 01690 710534 or visit www.guesthouse-snowdonia.co.uk

Portmeirion

A Mediterranean-style, follyesque village built on the Atlantic coast by Clough Williams-Ellis, who also designed the Snowdon summit café. This fascinating, fun place has a feel to it that is a cross between Monte Carlo and Disneyland.
It was here that the cult series The Prisoner was filmed. A splendid, if surreal, spot to visit or stay. Call 01766 770000 or visit www.portmeirion.wales.com

Visit here

Alternative Technology

The Centre for Alternative Technology is a charity that aims to "inspire, inform, and enable" people to live more sustainably. It's a great place to find solutions to everyday environmental problems, including renewable energy, and environmental building.
Call 01654 705950 or visit www.cat.org.uk

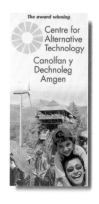

Aber Falls

The Aber Falls is one of the finest cascades in Wales. It is situated above the neighbouring village of Abergwyngregyn on the north Wales coast. Walks around the falls, some 30 minutes or so from the car park (grid ref SH664719), offer great views across the Menai Straits.

More information

Snowdonia National Park, *call 01766 770274 or visit www.eryri-npa.gov.uk*

Snowdonia Weather Service, *call 09068 500449*

Snowdonia and North Wales Tourism, *visit www.snowdonia-information.co.uk*

Lake District legends

In Cumbria every lake, every village, every footpath has a story to tell.
Perry Cleveland-Peck discovers 12 tales (and trails) of the unexpected.
Pictures: Matthew Roberts

Annan

Carlisle

Solway Firth

5

4

2

Whitehaven

10 Keswick

6

3

Ullswater

11

7

a. Wainwright

9

1

Coniston Water

8 12

Kendal

Barrow-in-Furness

Morecombe

N

Getting there... and made it!
Arduous and beautiful as Wainwright said. His writing made the climb to Dove Crag legendary.

Walk 1: On the wings of a dove

Perhaps the most legendary Lake District individual, as far as the walker is concerned, is Alfred Wainwright. The walker, writer and artist is famous for his guides to this much loved area of the country and is celebrated the world over. Fifty years ago Wainwright returned from a walk to Dove Crag near Fairfield and put pen to paper, writing the first words of The Eastern Fells, his debut guidebook.

It's half a century later and Matthew, Country Walking's photographer, and I set off for Dove Crag in memory and celebration of our hero. It is a foggy morning and we're both feeling a little jaded, having got up at 4.30am to drive to the Lakes. Neither of us feel particularly inclined to take on this awkward, low-visibility climb to the summit of Red Screes – I think we'd both prefer to kip in the car. But if Alfred did it, so can we.

Today the fog is something of a blessing. It lies so thick on the air that making out the summit of Red Screes is impossible from our starting point near the aptly-named Ambleside road, The Struggle, and we are able to kid ourselves as we set off that our goal is just tantalisingly above the next layer of damp, clotted air overhead.

It doesn't take great feats of imagination to see why this fell is called Red Screes. While the path at the base is firm and sure, we soon hit patches of loose purple and red stones as we make our way up the Kilnshaw Chimney. The scree wears us out rapidly, the rhythm of our steps disrupted as our feet slide about beneath us. Occasionally the awkward shifting terrain turns to more stable rock and something of a scramble is involved.

We make the summit and take a breather at the trig point – both of us yet to enjoy a single glimpse of the glorious fells and dales of the landscape we both so enjoy. But then, as we head north west towards Broad Crag the fog tears open and the great ridges and valleys of the Fairfield Horseshoe are revealed, like invisible giants materialising before our very eyes. North west lies the mighty Helvellyn. Magnificent. In the valley below sits Brotherswater, winking in the halflight behind clouds beneath us.

To our right, the east, the folds and ridges of High Street run off to the distance – another legendary walk we plan to make. Just a few moments of this privileged view is enough to recharge any walker's batteries. We set off once more with a new found spring in our steps and with all memories of jadedness well and truly banished.

By the time we get around Little Hart Crag and make our way to the top of Dove Crag, the fog has rolled in again.

Occasional glimpses of Ambleside and Windermere in the valley below is all that's on offer now. But the solitude that comes with the mist seems oddly suitable for our pilgrimage and as we admire the cairn at Dove Crag we do it with the words of our hero Alfred Wainwright echoing around our minds,
"It will be arduous, but the reward will be well worth the work."

The Route

Distance: *8km/5 miles*
Start: *There are circular routes to Dove Crag from Ambleside or Red Screes. From Red Screes (grid ref NY402081) head up Kilnshaw Chimney and over Broad Crag, crossing Scandale Pass and heading north west around base of Little Hart Crag (grid ref NY373108) to Dove Crag. Head down Dovedale to Hartshop Hall then pick up Caiston Glen path south to Scandale Pass. Head east back to Red Screes.*

Walk 2: Roaming Romans

Perry displays the self-discipline of a centurion along the Roman road

"We recreate the Roman experience by walking in the footsteps of the legions."

The Route

Distance: 7km/41/2 miles
Start: Park at Pooley Bridge (grid ref NY471244). Walk through village and head up the road until it becomes a track. Pick up High Street Roman Road to The Cockpit (grid ref NY483223). Take path heading north east and then pick up path to Heughscar Hill. Take path descending north past Heugh Scar. Pick up path heading left back to original track.

The regulation Roman army marching rate was 20 miles in five hours. Having just climbed Dove Crag, there's little chance that Matt and I are going to maintain that pace this afternoon. But we are out to enjoy some kind of Roman experience by walking in the footsteps of the legions, across the mountains between Penrith and Ambleside.

Or parts of them, at least. We park at Pooley Bridge on the northern shore of Ullswater and head up the track to Heughscar Hill. The fog has all but burnt away now and there are some great views over the lake and its wooded banks below us. A smooth white limestone track that runs through the fell heather makes for a refreshing change after the scree and we soon reach a cairn that marks the spot where the High Street Roman Road descends from Loadpot Hill to cross our track.

A little further on and we stumble upon The Cockpit, a stone circle built into a raised bank, much older than the road beside it. We sit by the stones for a while drinking in the scenery – Blencathra watches us broodingly over the lower hills to the west while Helvellyn provides the majestic backdrop to Ullswater. Above us, a pair of kestrels take on a lone buzzard in some feathered gladiatorial sport.

From the Cockpit the Roman Road heads north to the site of an ancient Roman fort (Brocavum) beneath Brougham Castle. A mile or so south west of Brougham are two circular monuments, or henges. One of them, King Arthur's Round Table, is actually a Bronze Age monument, though local legend has it that Sir Lancelot killed a giant there. You can't follow the course of the Roman road to Penrith but you can get to Brougham Castle and the henges by taking a path from the Cockpit to Askham and then north along the banks of the River Lowther.

Today, however, I am happy to be amused with the thought of all those fast-walking Italians roaming about this hillside so many centuries ago. But not so much that I fail to notice the rumble in my stomach. In keeping with the afternoon's theme Matt and I decide that some pasta is called for and head off back to the car. Ciao!

Walk 3: Lonesome Wanderings

Aira Force is a jaw-dropping 80ft waterfall on the banks of Ullswater. In the 1780s the Howard family of Greystoke Castle landscaped the area around the waterfall, and used it as a pleasure garden, planting more than half a million native and ornamental trees, and establishing a network of leafy tracks, footpaths and bridges – the very tracks, in fact, that I am enjoying today, thanks to the National Trust. It is a beautiful spot that is inspiring to anyone – walkers, horticulturalists or, indeed, writers.

A certain William Wordsworth used the valley of Aira Beck as the setting of his poem The Somnambulist, a romantic, tragic legend about a girl whose lover is away on a crusade. The poet, who celebrates his bicentenary this year, was also moved to write another ode after a walk along this part of Ullswater, which begins with the famous line "I wandered lonely as a cloud". We recommend that you do the same – though you'll be lucky to find any daffodils in November.

The Route

Distance: *6km/4 miles*
Start: *Go early. Park at the National Trust car park on the A5091 (grid ref NY399205 – the other National Trust one on the A592 costs money). Enjoy waterfall and take path following Aira Beck downstream. Take path heading east through Gowbarrow Park and Swinburn Park to the farm track at Underwood. Head west along country road. Take road on left to Ulcat Row (grid ref NY416235). Pick up footpath that veers south back to Aira Force.*

Walk 4: Smash hit

Believe it or not, but this little ditty was as big as Michael Jackson's Thriller in its heyday. It is the first verse of an English hunting song, dating from shortly before the middle of the 19th century. The hero was a Cumberland farmer, who kept a pack of fox hounds. The words of the song are by his friend John Woodcock Graves.

According to local lore, both men met one night at Graves' house. The grandmother of Graves' children was singing a child to sleep with an old nursery rhyme known as Bonnie Annie, and Graves was struck by the idea of writing a song for his hunting pal to the same tune. He completed it before Peel left the house and jokingly remarked "By Jove, Peel, you'll be sung when we are both run to earth".

Little did he know. Peel died in 1854, aged seventy-eight. The song went on to become a massive hit for more than a century, playing in dance halls as far away as Tasmania. John Peel went platinum!

The 70-mile Cumbria Way runs from Ulverston on the shores of Morecambe Bay to Carlisle, taking in Coniston Water, Langdale Valley, Borrowdale and Caldbeck, Peel's hometown. It offers some of the finest scenery of the area – scenery that would have been familiar to Peel as he rode to hounds.

We choose a length of the path that runs alongside the River Caldew near Mosedale. The heady, earthy smell of bracken hangs on the evening air, the last of the sunlight illuminating the purple heather on the flanks of Carrock Fell. And as I sit by the river a lone rider goes by us, the rhythm of the horse's footsteps seemingly in time with the tumbling Caldew water.

The Route

Distance: *8km/5 miles*
Start: *The 72-mile Cumbria Way runs from Ulverston to Carlisle. Park near the Meeting House Tea Rooms in Mosedale (grid ref NY357322). Walk along the banks of the Caldew to the Cumbria Way. Return for tea.*

*D'ye ken John Peel with his coat so gray,
D'ye ken John Peel at the break of day,
D'ye ken John Peel when he's far away,
With his hounds and his horn in the morning.*

Walk 5: Round in circles

This magical circle of thirty-eight stones is well worth a visit, not only to see the forms and textures of this ancient monument but also to admire the sensibility with which the Bronze Agers chose this lovely site. A good time to visit is after dawn or at dusk, although it's accessible at all times.

This morning, Matt and I have Castlerigg to ourselves. The setting is indeed awesome, the green mosses and lichens on the stones a reflection of the vast, unspoilt space around us. The circle is, in effect, within a vast natural amphitheatre formed by the surrounding hills – Skiddaw to the north and the Derwent Fells to the east – across which the shadows of the passing clouds provide a kaleidoscopic backdrop.

Nothing is really known about this site. In 1875 a stone axe was found here and it's now in Keswick Museum. Some excavation was carried out in 1882, in the rectangular grouping of stones that join the eastern side. Bizarrely, only charcoal was found. The mystery of Castlerigg makes it all the more enchanting – go and bewitch yourself.

The Route

Distance: *8km/5 miles*
Start: *Park at Castlerigg lay-by (grid ref NY293237). Pick up footpath that runs south from the bottom of the stone circle. Head south to High Nest then east to Low Rigg. Head north up and over Low Rigg to disused quarries (grid ref NY307237). Pick up road to Naddle Bridge and then footpath back to car park.*

Mysterious stones at Castlerig

122

Walk 6: Suprise view

The Victorians were a peculiar bunch. While you and I are quite happy to bimble up and down the fells to drink in the glorious views, this experience was too intense for our forefathers, who preferred their vistas a little more, well, refined.So Victorian tourists borrowed from the science of optics a device they felt would edit out all the savage sights of nature in the raw and offer up picturesque images of the Lakes, as swept out before them.

Or behind them, actually, as the device in question was a small black mirror. It was no ordinary mirror, of course, but was a plano-convex mirror or "Claude Glass". It would reflect Lake District panoramas in sepia to make it look like a work by landscape artist Claude Lorraine.

Yes, just a few generations ago, our ancestors would travel all the way to the Lake District with a guide that provided details of compatible views, or "stations", as they were known, only to stand with their backs to the sights.

So, in the interest of history, or perhaps deep, uncharted British eccentricity, Matt and I set out to find some of these stations. And while plano-convex mirrors are a little hard to come by these days, I have brought a regular mirror along.

I've been assured by travel writer and Country Walking contributor Paddy Dillon, that Friar's Crag on the banks of Derwent Water and Surprise View, above it, are two of the Victorian viewpoints. A third is at Claife Heights above Windermere.

The real surprise about Surprise View is that it is no surprise. To anyone. When I roll up with my mirror, it's apparent that the place is well known to quite a number of people. I try to explain what I'm doing with my back to this panorama and I offer to give people a go on my mirror. For some reason they are all obliged to depart, rather quickly, for less surprising places.

Which means I can dump the mirror and enjoy having the view all to myself. Perhaps those Victorians were on to something after all.

The Route

Distance: *4km/21/2 miles*
Start: *There are numerous parking spaces on the Watendlath road off the B5289 on the eastern shore of Derwent Water. We suggest you park at the bottom and walk up to Surprise View (grid ref NY279189), passing over the charming Ashness Bridge, a walk which is about 2km there, 2km back.*

Walk 7: Professor of adventure

The Route

Distance: *5.3km/3¼ miles*
Start: *Park at Rosthwaite car park (grid ref NY258147). Head west down track to Derwent. Cross via stones or bridge. Pick up Allerdale Ramble running north along river through Borrowdale to Broadslack Gill. At sign turn left, leaving Derwent and head south to where path meets Tongue Gill. Head east to Rosthwaite.*

One of the more eccentric legends of the lakes involves a man called Millican Dalton, known as the "Professor of Adventure". The Prof was a former London shipping clerk of the Thirties who gave up the rat race to return to his one true love – the mountains. He lived in a cave on the flanks of Castle Crag near Borrowdale and made his own clothes. Pop into any of the many tea rooms in the area and the chances are you'll see a picture of him looking splendidly quirky on board his home-made sailing raft.

Now anyone who calls themselves Professor of Adventure is a man I can relate to. I just have to see the place where this great individual dwelt. And as Borrowdale, with its thickly wooded valleys, tumbling becks and glassy river pools, just happens to be one of my favourite walking areas of the Lake District, well, I can see myself getting on with the ghost of the professor like a cave on fire.

I set off from the car park at the sleepy village of Rosthwaite and head through a farm and down a track to the ford and over the stepping stones on the River Derwent there. Across the Derwent and there are any number of routes to Castle Crag, including the Cumbria Way and the Allerdale Ramble. In my eagerness, I opt for the path that bears right through a field and up to the Crag directly.

I have with me a compass and my Ordnance Survey Outdoor Leisure map with details of the caves around Castle Crag. And I have with me some water and a little food. The only thing I don't have is the exact location of the professor's cave. Hmmm.

This talentless undergraduate of adventure searches high and low for the Professor's cave. I search under banks of bracken, behind mossy piles of slate from the disused quarry above Castle Crag and between the trees of High and Low Hows Wood. Then I find a cave, which momentarily makes my heart race until I realise that the entrance bears no inscription and sadly, is not the one I'm after.

Despite buckets of perspiration and a few choice words from Matt, Dalton's cave eludes me (I know, Professor, I must try harder). So, while I return to much-needed study at the University of Grid Reference, this legend of the lakes lives on unseen. But half the fun of the Professor of Adventure's cave is in the finding.
Go try it yourself.

Perhaps this is the way to the Professor of Adventure's cave......

Walk 8: Bluebirds & Swallows

The Route

Distance: 5.6km/31/2 miles

Start: Park in Torver. Take footpath (grid ref SD286945) to Brackenbarrow Farm and Torver Common Wood, Head south along shore of Coniston and then south west across Torver Beck (grid ref SD2892) to reservoir. Head north back to Torver.

Coniston is perhaps most famous for its connection with Sir Donald Campbell's ill-fated world water-speed record attempt in 1967. In his boat Bluebird, Campbell had already set a record of 202.32mph on Ullswater in 1955, then 276.3mph on Lake Dumbeyung in 1966. On his final attempt on January 4 1967, timekeepers recorded a speed of 318mph before Bluebird, just a few metres from the final buoy, climbed into the air, somersaulted and vanished beneath the waters. Sir Donald's body and the wreck of Bluebird were recovered by divers only recently.

Standing on the shores of Coniston, you can't help but think of the legendary nature of Campbell's efforts. But, today, as a small yacht goes by, it is another nautical tale that seems to better fit the peaceful mood of the place. Coniston is also the setting for Arthur Ransome's much loved children's book Swallows and Amazons. And while the place names in the book are different, for those in the know you can soon work out where each of the stories were set. Peel Island is the site of the Secret Harbour and Wild Cat Island, the River Crake is the Amazon, Allan Tarn is Octopus Lagoon and the Old Man of Coniston himself is Kanchenjunga.

> "Standing on the shores of Coniston, you can't help but think of the legendary nature of Campbell's efforts."

Walk 9: Gingerbread

Grasmere has a number of legendary figures attached to it. The celebrated English novelist Thomas De Quincey, famous for his Confessions of an Opium Eater, lived at Nab Cottage there. The "Lake poet" William Wordsworth and his sister Dorothy lived for 50 years at Dove Cottage nearby. Samuel Taylor Coleridge and Sir Walter Scott were regular visitors to their homes.

But if Wordsworth, De Quincey and friends provide legends to feed the mind, my particular Grasmere favourite feeds the stomach. Take a stroll past St Oswald's churchyard of a morning and your nostrils will be assailed by the most delightfully sweet, spicy, buttery aroma that spells (or is it smells?) out only one thing – the world famous gingerbread of Sarah Nelson – a rather scary-looking old bird if the image on the greaseproof packaging is anything to go by. Follow your nose to a little cottage in the wall of the churchyard for the ultimate walker's treat – a packet of six of these golden brown gastronomic treasures placed strategically at the top of a rucksack before a day out on the fells will see you up and down any incline with a smile on your face and a glow in your belly. They have been doing so for walkers since 1854.

For more information call 01539 435428 or visit www.grasmeregingerbread.co.uk

Walk 10: Squirrel walk

The most legendary Lakeland author is surely Beatrix Potter, whose most famous character, Peter Rabbit, celebrated his centenary recently. Her home at Hill Top and a museum about her work at Hawkshead are both extremely popular tourist attractions, and best steered clear of by the discerning walker. However, you can get a feel for the landscape that so inspired the writer, and you can avoid hoards of Potter fans by taking in a stroll around Derwent Water. It was here that she set her Tale of Squirrel Nutkin, and, if you're as lucky as I was, you might just see one of the red squirrels that are unusually common here.

Above: Look for the carving inside a split boulder at Calfclose Bay
Below: Squirrel Nutkin is alive and well at Derwent Water

Friar's Crag, a promontory on the eastern bank of Derwent Water, is on a stretch of shore John Ruskin described as having "one of the three or four most beautiful views in Europe". It's called Friar's Crag because it is believed to be the embarkation point for monks making a pilgrimage to St Herbert's Island, where the saint – and, incidentally, where Old Brown from Squirrel Nutkin – was said to live.

On the northern shore of Calfclose Bay, keen-eyed walkers may spot an unusual split boulder (grid ref NY267215). Go and investigate the polished sculpture inside the boulder, commemorating 100 years of The National Trust. Like Ruskin, Potter played a key role in the trust.

The Route

Distance: *12km/7 1/2 miles*
Start: *Park at car park (grid ref NY265229) north of Friar's Crag. Follow path south to Calfclose Bay. Cross Borrowdale Road and head north east through the Great Wood to Castlerigg. Head north west to Castlehead Wood and then take path west back to car.*

Mark Hamblin

125

Walk 11: Beauty of Buttermere

If Lake Buttermere has a beauty all of its own, Lake Buttermere also has a *Beauty* all of its own. It was thrust into the full glare of media attention in 1792 when a Joseph Budworth published a guidebook, A Fortnight's Ramble in the Lakes. In the book Budworth went into raptures about the beauty of the local innkeeper's daughter, Mary Robinson. Mary became a tourist attraction herself.

In 1802, the Honourable Colonel Alexander Augustus Hope, MP for Linlithgow, arrived in Buttermere for some char fishing, and promptly swept young Mary off her feet. They were married within weeks. All would have gone well for Alexander and Mary, except that Alexander was not actually Alexander. The supposed MP was in fact a notorious swindler, bigamist and impostor by the name of James Hatfield.

When one Samuel Taylor Coleridge, Keswick correspondent for London's Morning Post, filed his story on the marriage, Hatfield was found out and there was an outcry. Hatfield was arrested.

He managed a daring escape but was caught again and eventually hanged – not for the bigamy but for impersonating an MP, something that was considered a very serious crime in those days (we at CW can't imagine anyone wanting to impersonate an MP today). Mary remarried in 1808 and died in 1837. She is buried in Caldbeck churchyard.

The bizarre tale was almost immediately taken up by writers and playwrights. Wordsworth praised Mary's virtue in his poem The Prelude. The latest contributor to the genre is Melvyn Bragg, whose book The Maid of Buttermere was published in 1987. You too can participate in this particular legend. The Fish Inn still sits on the banks of the Buttermere, though now it is the Fish Hotel. For more information call 017687 70253 or visit www.fish-hotel.co.uk. Oh, and did I mention the beauty of the landlord's daughter?

> Beauty of Buttermere
> .... *unfaithful to a virtuous wife,*
> *Deserted and deceived, the Spoiler came*
> *And wooed the artless daughter of the hills*
> *And wedded her, in cruel mockery*
> *Of love and marriage bonds....*

The Route

Distance: *6.4km/4 miles*
Start: *There is a footpath running around Buttermere. But make the diversion to Low Raven Crag (grid ref NY195147) south of Gatesgarth farm on the southern end of Buttermere for fantastic views.*

Scandal, bigamy and fraud came to Buttermere – all for the love of a beautiful innkeeper's daughter.

Walk 12: Brantwood

John Ruskin, considered the philosophical father of The National Trust, lived at Brantwood on the eastern bank of Coniston water between 1872 and his death in 1900. During his time there Brantwood became an intellectual powerhouse and one of the greatest artistic and literary centres in Europe. Ruskin's home is now owned by the trust and the 250 acres of gardens and estate are open to walkers, and feature a fantastic walk to Crag Head with routes into the Grizedale Forest behind Brantwood.

For more information call 01539 441396 or visit www.brantwood.org.uk

Get philosophical as you look out at Coniston from Brantwood and you'll be in great company.

Before you go...

Maps:

Ordnance Survey Explorers OL4, OL5, OL6 and OL7.
Harvey Maps Lakeland North, West, Central, East, South West and South East

Stay here:

The Rothay Garden Hotel, Grasmere, tel 01539 435334.
The New Dungeon Ghyll Hotel, Great Langdale, tel 01539 437213.

Highs and lows of the Lake District

From heart-thumping hikes along Helvellyn's Striding Edge to blissful strolls through Borrowdale, Lake District national park has much to offer walkers of all abilities.

Words: **Richard Baker, Perry Cleveland-Peck, Jonathan Manning, Marianne Powell**
Pictures: **Tom Bailey, Matthew Roberts, Neil Hepworth, Trevor Rickwood**

Highs and lows. In many learned circles these two terms are mutually exclusive, denoting, for instance, the fair and foul days of weather forecasts, the boom and bust of economic markets, or the violent mood swings of manic depressives.

When it comes to us walkers, however, highs and lows can be combined to create a scintillating outdoors experience, offering new perspectives on our favourite landscapes, not to mention weekends of towering adventure and gentle relaxation.

To celebrate this plurality, we decided to go high, to the very tops of England no less, and then compare and contrast the trails, landscape and views there with low-level walking nearby. Think of it as the yin and yang of walking.

We've chosen three of the Lake District's best-known peaks – Helvellyn, Skiddaw and Scafell – and three of the area's most rich and beautiful valleys – Eskdale, Langdale and Borrowdale – and investigated the most rewarding routes on offer. The objective is to offer you three different weekends of walking, a high and a low for each. But whether you try our combinations or mix and match them is entirely up to you.

However, a word to the wise. It's no accident that we are visiting these high grounds in the height of summer. While the mountain tops are mostly pleasantly cool at this time of year, they can still bite. So pack waterproofs, a spare fleece and hat and gloves, something to eat and drink on your journey, and a map and compass, of course. Please don't think about trying these routes in winter unless you're very experienced. It's important to bear in mind that while we walkers may occasionally like to have our heads in the clouds, our feet should remain firmly on the ground. So take care and enjoy.

Heading for the southern shore of Derwent Water on a walk through Borrowdale.

129

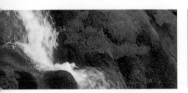

Skiddaw

With its clear footpaths and easy terrain, this is a mountain that just about anyone can walk up.

We take the Allerdale Ramble route up Carl Side, a path as wide as a car, from which only four buffoons could stray in good weather. If, like us, you do stray, the precipitous route up Slades Beck is wonderfully quiet and you'll have only waterfalls, surprised sheep, buzzards, pipits and ring ouzels as company.

Skiddaw's sheep are award winners. On the eastern side of the mountain, a memorial stands as testament to turn-of-the-century shepherds who tended flocks of the highest quality. And hefted stock such as theirs carries its genes down through the generations. So, if the sheep do look a little haughty when you pass, they've every right.

The team are in fine fettle. Our steeper-than-

> "For me, this is one of the most wonderful sights in Lakeland. And I'm not alone. The summit plateau is wide and gentle, but without exception, and with all points of the compass available, every summiteer is slugging back tea and juice with an eye only for the east."

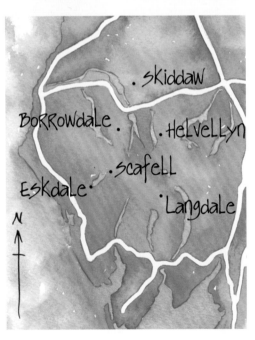

To 'bag'. A crude verb, slightly dismissive. Can indicate a number of actions, including to shoot geese, be bowled out for two ducks, or to imprison crisps. But, in the parlance of walkers, it means to have reached the summit of a mountain, and to be looking forward to the next challenge.

Yet Skiddaw is not a mountain you should 'bag'. Ease your way to the fourth highest summit in Lakeland by all means, but in so doing take the time to admire what is Keswick's adventure playground, a 24-hour massif. Upon every chime someone on its slopes is doing something different.

Nicola, Neil, Perry and I begin our walk above Keswick at Millbeck, on a dizzily blue-skied day.

planned ascent is chalked off with barely a wheeze. Step into a steady rhythm and just keep going – stop at each likely corner in the path and turn around to enjoy forever views – take a swig or two of water, the reward of a biscuit now and then. And on, higher. And higher. The paths are crumbly and dusty but our boots' grip rarely fails on what is the oldest rock in Cumbria, slate born out of ancient seas.

Two easy hours see us to Carlside Tarn, at the top of Slades Beck, which is Skiddaw's major junction, where walkers meet after rambles up bony Ullock Pike and stagger across from Little Man. From here the grassed way turns to scree, and the lung exercise begins in earnest for the short haul to the top.

We stop to imagine the mountain at night. Moonlit ascents are not uncommon, especially in summer, and the tarn is an excellent place to rest and wait for the dawn. With Keswick bustling below, its B&Bs filling nicely, Perry remarks how, as the terrain is not difficult, almost anyone could have a go, and what an adventure it would be to leave the warmth of your duvet and begin a climb at the witching hour.

Skiddaw House Youth Hostel is one of the most remote dwellings in England. Originally built as a shooting lodge 100 years ago (there are grouse butts dug into the fells all around) it was later used as a shepherd's bothy, and is now a youth hostel, the highest in England, albeit one closed during 2003 as a lack of funds threatens its existence.

We explore for as long as it takes to eat an apple, and then our world is joined by a train of mountain bikers. "Thankyouuuu!" they smile as they hurtle by. We are heading along Lonscale fellside and shadows are being cast over our path. Above, a great canopy of red silk suspends a man in the sky. He drifts up and down on the whim of the wind. Imagine that...

On we head, completing our circle, by old mine workings and the excesses of mineralogists, who have picked and prised the rare strata here for 500 years, and on to the Tourist Path. This is the more sedate, eastern route to Skiddaw's top. Victorians used to make languid progress up it, often on a pony, as far as the refreshment (or temperance) huts that stood on the way. Whereupon most felt giddy and returned.

Here, too, a wholly daft event used to take place. It is a very English act to drive a car up a grass slope until it can go no further. And on Skiddaw it has been happening for years, firstly with Austin 7s (one made it to the top in 1960). Now the local motor club invites more or less any car to have a go on nearby farmland. Meanwhile, Skiddaw probably sighs deeply inside, but she has suffered greater indignities at the hands of miners.

This walk is a long one, and when we reach the car, we crumple a little, lie on the floor and peer up at the summit.

To 'sag'. It means you are, quite frankly, knackered – but you've had a fabulous time.

Nicola has her mind on a sunlit top, however, and views that, on a clear day, take in Derwent Water, Bassenthwaite Lake, the Uldale Fells and pierce deep into the southern mountains. Best of all, though, is what you find to the east. Skiddaw's Empty Quarter, a precious wilderness where there isn't a road or house in sight, and your mobile phone can only bleep its impotence. The Cumbria Way bisects this enormous grassy bowl, which gathers below Blencathra, Bowscale Fell and Mungrisedale Common.

For me, this is one of the most wonderful sights in Lakeland. And I'm not alone. The summit plateau is wide and gentle, but without exception, and with all points of the compass available, every summiteer is slugging back tea and juice with an eye only for the east.

Silence descends, and it feels great to step off the rock and pace across the spongy fell. From 3,053ft, the way home is circuitous, a gentle trail, but we still feel like frontiersmen, stepping into the Big Country, a fiery crucible of golden grass and umber heather.

The Route

Skiddaw, via Carl Side
Terrain: *Good rock paths, grassy fell, some road.*
Route: *From lay-by (grid ref NY255263) follow Allerdale Ramble path through fields beside river. Track west towards Dodd, then go north up ridge of Carl Side. At Carlside Tarn the track is joined by Allerdale Ramble route along Ullock Pike and Longside Edge. Head to summit. Track back from here on south-easterly bridleway towards Little Man, but at fence crossing, veer east towards youth hostel. From here follow Cumbria Way south on track hugging Lonscale Fell, around shoulder to face Latrigg with Derwent Water beyond. At car park, take road downhill through Applethwaite, on to Millbeck and the start.*
Map:
Ordnance Survey Explorer OL4, Harvey Superwalker Lakeland North.
Distance: *15.5km/9¾ miles.*
Time: *6 hours.*

Borrowdale

Crossing the wild landscape towards Dock Tarn

Caffle
House
Tearoom
The 5th
Generation

HOT & COLD
REFRESHMENTS.
HOME BAKING.
CONFECTIONERY.

Occasionally, rarely, the great poker game of life deals us a royal flush, and as the early sun warms our backs while we lace our boots, it's hard to think of a hand that would beat the cards we're holding today. Where the circuit of Buttermere might score a pair of aces, and the ascent of Skiddaw three kings, today's unbeatable hand includes cards for Borrowdale, Derwent Water, Watendlath and Dock Tarn.

You would need a hand of a dozen cards and a pack with a score of aces to convey the beauty and variety of this trail, as it heads by woodland, fell, river, beck, lake, moorland, mountain and valley. So, with Skiddaw cutting an impressive silhouette on the horizon, we leave Rosthwaite and skip across stepping-stones over the River Derwent. Today the river is little more than a narrow stream, but the stones somehow mark a magical entry to Borrowdale.

> Woodland, fell, beck, moor and mountain – when it comes to walking, this really is a big deal.

We turn right through High and then Low Hows Wood, the river never far from our side and a mocking woodpecker rapping a tree without ever disclosing its location. The clear path and regular fingerposts to Grange mean navigation is easy, so we confine our maps to pockets and admire the cliffs up to our right, painted on the skyline with broad Van Gogh brush strokes.

The sun is already high as we enter Grange, and with fleeces swiftly stored we inspect the spooky tombstone-shaped slates that serve as an effective churchyard wall.

Leaving the village, we soon head east on a path that rises to a platform along the southern shores of Derwent Water, like a giant Scalextric track. We step down to take a close look at three toads in the reeds. With neither the charm nor the fairytale promise of frogs, the toads remain unkissed, and we head up to the B5289 and turn right.

If the walk so far has been relaxingly level, the path we climb to High Lodore is lung-burstingly steep. Fortunately, it's also relatively short, and 15 minutes later we're basking in midday sun by a drystone wall as we settle for lunch. It's tempting to stay longer, but Watendlath Beck lies ahead, and we're soon enjoying the shade as we explore the woodland, before following the beck towards Watendlath down a perfect Lakeland valley.

The water is clear and smooth, like the bobbled surface of ancient window glass, and the beck leads us to Watendlath over a handsome cobbled packhorse bridge (although we can't find the stone laid by the Prince of Wales, apparently marked HRH CHARLES 22-5-95).

We push on alongside Watendlath Tarn, where the fly-fishermen seem to have the right idea, drifting in boats in the gentle breeze, teased by trout rising just out of casting range. Ignoring the packhorse trail ahead, we instead follow a route along the shoreline, with a tall drystone wall to our left, before climbing on a path that changes from a well-beaten track to a series of flagstones in the hillside, valuable no doubt in boggier times. Behind us, Watendlath nestles beautifully at the end of the tarn, sheltered in the basin of hills like a frontier family's homestead.

Our cameras restored to rucksacks, we follow fingerposts to Dock Tarn, and climb sharply into the first truly wild landscape of our walk, with the land disappearing over a cliff to our right. Just below the summit of Great Crag, Dock Tarn emerges to our left, a peaty oasis amid the rock and bracken. It's impossible to resist the temptation to stop and stare, the dark waters somehow stilling our beating hearts after the ascent. Ahead, low cloud has started to veil High Crag like an ungainly bride, while to our left Langstrathdale opens into the perfect U-shaped valley, as if a primary school teacher had carved the letter into the landscape.

A duckboard platform carries you over potentially boggy ground outside the village of Grange, near Derwent Water

But there's nothing childish about the descent from the summit. Flights of steps see us on hands and bums before crossing the footbridge for Stonethwaite, described by AW Wainwright as being 'most representative of the romantic charm of Lakeland'. We cross the river to follow the path back to Rosthwaite.

We've seen woodland, fell, river, beck, lake, moorland, mountain and valley on this walk. We've danced across stepping stones, strided along duckboards and savoured ice creams by the bejewelled surface of a tarn. And as we reach the car, we're sure that if this walk were a poker hand we could raise anyone's stake. It really is a royal flush of the Lakes.

> **"If this walk were a poker hand we could raise anyone's stake. It's a royal flush of the Lakes."**

The Route

Borrowdale and Watendlath
Terrain: *good paths, some steep climbs, boggy in parts.*
Route: *Leave car park in Rosthwaite (grid ref NY256148), turn Right and follow track to stepping stones over River Derwent. Turn R to Grange. Pass L through village, then 500m later take footpath R towards southern shore of Derwent Water, using platform over boggy ground. At B5289 turn R, then L on path 50m before hotel in Lodore. Climb hill through woodland to Watendlath Beck, and follow to Watendlath. Keep tarn on L and follow sign to Dock Tarn. Pass R shore of tarn, then follow path R to Stonethwaite. Follow road to B5289, cross towards hostel, then take path on corner R back to Rosthwaite.*
Map: *Ordnance Survey Explorer OL4, Harvey Superwalker Lakeland West.*
Distance: *16km/10miles.*
Time: *5 hours.*

Helvellyn

Prepare for the many personalities of the UK's favourite mountain.

The Route

Old Pony Route

Terrain: *Steep grass, fell, rocky ridge.*

Route: *From the car park at grid ref NY315168 pick up Helvellyn Gill path or head north to Thirlspot for Old Pony Route (over Whiteside Bank). Head south east to Helvellyn. Take Wythburn path south then west to Thirlmere. Pick up permissive path (NY327136) and head north to start.*

Maps: *Ordnance Survey Explorer OL5, Harvey Superwalker Lakeland Central.*

Distance: *9km/5½ miles.*

Time: *5 hours.*

Helvellyn. The word alone seems moody and sinister, enough to stir the heart of even the hardiest walker, like hiking to Hades or Valhalla. And for a long time Helvellyn was considered the most antisocial of all England's mountains. But how things change.

Today Helvellyn is the nation's favourite hill, scaled by enthusiasts from the ages of eight to 80.

This doesn't mean it should be taken lightly, of course – come winter and Helvellyn takes on a very different personality. But as with much in life, there is an easy way and a hard way to success on her slopes. And while the more demanding routes to the top are rewarding for their challenging nature and heart-thumping views, the less-taxing paths can provide an equally enriching high-altitude experience. Especially in June.

There are two sides to Helvellyn's character. On the one, the east, Helvellyn is a little like Bizet's Carmen – alluring, capricious, unpredictable, even deadly on occasions. On the other, the western side, Helvellyn is like Sir Edward Heath, conventional and hard work, sometimes grumbly but essentially steady and good-natured.

It is a simple thing to plan a day's walk to the top of Helvellyn and back sticking solely to the Sir Ted side of the mountain. You can take the Old Pony Route, a cart track beloved of our less-than-intrepid Victorian forefathers, to the summit and return via the Wythburn Path and the shores of Thirlmere. On a good day this is a long and satisfying circular walk if ever there was one, affording stunning views over nearby Grasmere and the Langdale valley beyond. Alternative westerly routes to the top include those along the White Stones Path and Helvellyn Gill.

Today, however, I have a spring in my step and a desire for some hardcore Carmen action. And to get

At Hole-in-the-Wall we get our first glimpse of Striding Edge, serrated and buckled like the splintered blade of some god-wielded battle sword as it twists and jumps to the cloud-masked summit ahead. It's time to re-fuel, we decide. No point in trying anything complicated in this poor visibility, and we're ravenous now anyway. At Low Spying How we sit and munch for a while, commenting on the marbling hues of Red Tarn below us as the clouds work their shadows upon it.

And it works out fine. In the summer, Striding Edge is easily walkable. Yes, you need a good head for heights, the sides of the ridge simply plummet

> "We get our first glimpse of Striding Edge, serrated and buckled like the splintered blade of some god-wielded battle sword."

a feel for what this diva really has to offer I'm heading for Helvellyn's top via Striding Edge, to prove to myself that this infamous route is not beyond the mettle of us Country Walkers. It's a wonderful day for a long walk. The skies are blue, the sun is fierce but, like the perfect gin and tonic, it is complemented with a breeze that just takes the edge off it.

I set out from Glenridding on the western shore of Ullswater with Tom, our photographer. We hug Glenridding Beck for a while, our boots catching on the polished, path-encroaching roots of the dappling sycamores beside us. The brandy-brown beck to our right hisses and tumbles over gargling rock and mossy moor stones, great locks of green weed washing in the currents like the tresses of some mystical nymph.

We break from the shade and begin the trudge to Birkhouse Moor via Little Cove. It's a steady climb on a good block and gravel path. But it's steep, rising more than 1,300ft in a little over a mile. This is a walk you want to take steadily, without too many pit-stops. Tom tells me of his own measure of speed, that if you can't talk when walking up a steep slope, then you're going too fast. It seems sensible advice, but I'm too out of breath to comment.

to the valley floor either side. And yes, you need fair weather behind you – ensure you check before you go. But an earthy footpath runs along the side of the edge, hardly more arduous than the trail by the beck earlier. And the views...the views just take your breath away. The hardest section of the walk is the last 100m to the top, where some care and the occasional hand is called for.

From the summit, we drop south on a footpath over the top of Comb Crags, then west to the Wythburn woods. It's steep, my knees are feeling it now, but the occasional twinge is more than assuaged by the sense of achievement coursing through my veins.

The Route

Striding Edge
Terrain: *Woodland, steep fell, narrow ridge, steep grass.*
Route: This is a linear route, so you'll have to arrange to be picked up. Don't try this route backwards. From car park (grid ref NY387169) follow Glenridding Beck west to Gillside. Follow path south west to Little Cove and continue to Hole-in-the-Wall. Check weather. Go west along Striding Edge to summit. Descend via Birk Side to Wythburn.
Maps: *Ordnance Survey Explorer OL5, Harvey Superwalker Lakeland Central.*
Distance: *10km/6¼ miles.*
Time: *5 hours.*

Right: The start of the long trudge from Glenridding Beck to Birkhouse Moor

Scafell

Steep and stubborn, especially after a big bacon breakfast.

Left:Scafell's hanging Cliffs' from Hollow Stones

The Route

Green How and Hard Rigg

Terrain: *Woodland, steep grassy fell, rocky summit.*
Route: *From camp site (grid ref NY182076) follow Lingmell Gill to Burnmoor Bridleway. Pick up permissive footpath (NY184070) and climb west over Rakehead Crag to Scafell. Pick up Hard Rigg path heading south west to Burnmoor Tarn, for bridleway north back to starting point.*
Map: *Ordnance Survey Explorer OL6, Harvey Superwalker Lakeland West.*
Distance: *11.4km/7 miles.*
Time: *5 hours.*

From Hollow Stones today, the cliffs ahead are cloaked in cloud and mist and seem to hang high in the air, a breath-taking mutation of the floating islands of Jonathan Swift's Gulliver's Travels.

While the scenery is awe-inspiring, the weather comes as little surprise. Local shepherds maintain that if you can't see nearby Great Gable, it's raining. And if you can see it, then it's going to rain – cute, but hardly what you'd describe as meteorological optimism. The rain is holding off for the minute, but the visibility is low to say the least.

Earlier it had all seemed so different. Tom and I had set out from the northern shore of Wast Water, the sun dancing off the tumbling falls of Lingmell Gill, swathes of marsh marigold carpeting the banks in deep, vibrant yellow. A skylark's distinctive call played high on the morning air. We stopped to admire the arthritic, gnarled roots of an ancient oak, seeming to reach down with its creaking wooden limbs to gently guide the sparkling stream along its meandering journey.

There are few words needed to describe the climb to Scafell. 'Steep' is one of them. Today, on a breakfast ever so slightly fuller than was absolutely necessary, I'd like to throw in a 'relentless' as well.

You have to keep your wits about you. Tom and I had planned on taking the Green How Path to the top, returning by Hard Rigg. But what with one bacon rasher and another we seem to have missed a trick, and the hanging cliffs of Hollow Stones appear out of the mist ahead of us. Hmmm.

Scafell's summit is strewn with scree, stones and pebbles. When you reach it, don't be seduced by the more extravagant cairn at Symonds Knott – the summit of Scafell itself is just a little further south east, which is where Tom and I enjoy our high-altitude lunch in glorious solitude.

The westerly routes down from the top are obvious – I'm surprised we missed them on the way up. The Hard Rigg Path is clearly discernable as it stretches away to Burnmoor Tarn on Scafell's grassy south west flanks. Tom and I opt for the more direct, if discreet, Green How Path, which bears off Hard Rigg in a more westerly direction (look for the cairns).

The scree soon turns to undulating, bouncy grass, chewed vacantly by the resident Lakeland sheep, damp and aromatic, and decidedly non-plussed by our momentary intrusion from out of the clouds. And then the fellside levels out on Green How before plunging us over Rakehead Crag and down to the car.

Above: Skelwith Force, between the villages of Skelwith Bridge and Elterwater

"Scafell's summit is strewn with scree, stones and pebbles. Don't be seduced by the more extravagant cairn at Symonds Knott."

Langdale

Cavernous caves, crashing cascades, 5,000-year-old rock art and some Grasmere gingerbread for tea.

'No pain, no gain.' Has there ever been a more ridiculous phrase? In the world of walking, at least, gains can frequently be made without any pain at all. This walk to Rydal Water, for example, requires small effort but brings huge rewards. If you like the idea of classic Lakeland vistas without huge ascents, this may be the perfect route to ease you into your walking weekend.

We start from Grasmere, near the home of its most famous local boy, one William Wordsworth. It is said that Wordsworth walked more than 180,000 miles in his lifetime, and this comes as little surprise as the area sits amid countless inspirational views.

Today Perry, and I head west up a moderate incline over Raven Crag, where docile sheep outnumber the walkers, to Chapel Stile. Perhaps the crowds are put off by the dark scars of the quarrying, choosing to boycott a landscape that is more robust than picturesque. More fool them, for the beauty is in the detail here, such as the pale green lichen that clings to lumps of grey slate.

From one quarry to another as we look at the recently discovered ancient rock art near Chapel Stile, truly valuable marks carved on volcanic rock (find them at grid ref NY317054).

Prehistoric people journeyed from afar to use stones from the nearby Pike of Sickle for axes, and these drawings marked the way, showing the site was a special place. Axes were important status symbols in a time before metal – a stone-age version of a Rolex if you like – so the quarry here was of prime importance. Expert Stan Beckensall called these 5,000-year-old markings the 'rock art discovery of the decade' and the evidence of our ancient forefathers' existence can't fail to send a shiver down the spine.

We dodge crowds on the Cumbria Way before wending our way to Loughrigg Tarn. These days there's not much chance of wandering lonely as a cloud, but the peaceful, enclosed tarn successfully fools you into believing you have the region to yourself.

A short climb later and we are alone on Loughrigg Fell, surveying our route from on high. There are paths everywhere, but we follow one that leads you neatly on to the caves above Rydal Water. These dark, eerie openings look like the setting for a scene from Lord Of The Rings, and the rock is dark and rugose, inviting you to reach out and touch the textured walls. The enclosed space is quite a contrast to the wide expanses of sky that Scafell has to offer, but proves pleasantly cool on this summer stroll.

From the caves we head back to Grasmere along Loughrigg Terrace and the path beyond. This long, gentle route takes you past a stunning view of Grasmere lake, sparkling in the sunlight like a shoal of glass fish on the turn. So often, you walk for miles to reach a great view, only to spend the length of a tea break enjoying it. It makes a welcome change to take pleasure in such bewitching scenery for the entire length of the path – here the rusty orange heather of the hills, there the deep, calm black of the lake below.

But it's not long before we're back in Grasmere, where we sample some of its famous gingerbread before heading home and reflecting on a glorious day of no pain, and considerable gain.

The Route

Langdale
Terrain: *Varied, one rocky descent and some tricky sections to navigate.*
Route: *From Grasmere car park (grid ref NY338078) follow the road around to the Left, then take the first footpath on your R. Follow it to Chapel Stile and and the rock art, before descending to the B5343. From the road, head along the Cumbria Way. Follow this past Elter Water. Beyond waterfall nip back on to the road briefly, then take a path on your Left up to Loughrigg Tarn. Head Left around the tarn before striking out on the footpath up to Loughrigg Fell. Crossing the fell, you can skirt round the top, aiming for Nab Scar directly opposite, to bring you down near Rydal Water. Pass the caves, then follow Loughrigg Terrace above Grasmere lake before following the road back into Grasmere.*
Map: *Ordnance Survey Explorer OL7, Harvey Superwalker Central.*
Distance: *17km/11miles.*
Time: *6 hours.*

The spooky confines above Rydal Water.

Eskdale

A walk so delightful, we wanted to keep it all for ourselves.

A Country Walking journalist's lot can be a troublesome one. Don't get me wrong. It's not that we don't enjoy travelling around these islands of ours, sharing our bucolic adventures with you. But sometimes, just sometimes, we happen upon a stretch of countryside – a hidden dale, a secret copse – so unspoilt and heart-achingly handsome that we want it all to ourselves.

Selfish, I know. But so it was for me while en route to the Scafell massif to research said walk on these here pages. You see, I was all set on writing about a circular route around Buttermere to go with the Scafell climb, Buttermere being so elegant and dignified in contrast to the rugged trails that Scafell has to offer.

But getting to Scafell means travelling through Eskdale and Wasdale, and that's where the old plans went to pot. Tom and I turned on to the road that leads from Ambleside to Wasdale Head, and everything changed. The traffic seemed to disappear. The tourists evaporated. A blanket of pastoral tranquillity descended all around.

I'm not suggesting for one moment that these two valleys have never been written about before. Just wondering why I should contribute to the existing body of words, and encourage any more of you to spoil it for those of us in the know? So if you happen to be driving by High Birkhow, a little north of Nether Wasdale, be sure to keep on going!

For if you do locate the little-known permissive path that runs from a cattlegrid on the northern shore of Wast Water, past the youth hostel into Low Wood and on to the southern end of the lake, you'll be marring what I consider a personal gift the likes of which even the Prince of Wales' butler has never seen.

But none of this matters, because you'll have driven past it a long time ago. You certainly won't, for example, have spotted the gap at the south

The Route

Low Wood and Wast Water Lagoon
Terrain: *Woodland and lakeside paths.*
Route: *From the cattlegrid, at grid ref NY147048, follow permissive path south to Low Wood. Follow path south through wood to Lund Bridge. Cross river and head south east, then north east, to lagoon (NY145039). Return via same route. For longer walk return to bridge and head north west to Ashness How, then east along side of High Birkhow for road north back to cattlegrid. Adventurous walkers can try the circular around Wast Water via the path north from the lagoon beneath The Screes.*
Map: *Ordnance Survey Explorer OL6, Harvey Superwalker Lakeland West.*
Distance: *4.7km/3 miles.*
Time: *11/2 hours.*

> "On the map, the lagoon looks like a little teardrop, which is appropriate, because the panorama here is good enough to make you weep."

eastern corner of the youth hostel grounds that takes you into Low Wood, where oak and beech trees offer a shading canopy overhead, and pillowing rhododendrons tease you around every corner with beguiling half views. You won't have rested on Lund Bridge, a lolling packhorse crossing that stretches to a single sentinel oak that must be as old as the bridge itself. You won't have turned on to a dusty pink track and spotted the marigolds by the stream. You won't have passed a creaking boat house, for a secret lagoon at the southern shore of Wast Water itself.

On the map, the lagoon looks like a little teardrop, which is appropriate, because the panorama here is good enough to make you weep.

A view straight up the length of Wast Water, the distant Scafell range framed by The Screes on your right (a narrow path at the base carries you all the way to Wasdale Head) and the ripple-tickling fronds of a weeping willow on your left. Today, a haze has graced this glassy pool, lending the area an enchanted air. A buzzard wheels high in the summer sky, a flat pebble skips across the water.

But none of this really matters, because you'll have driven past a long time ago.

Before you go...

Stay here

Wasdale Head Inn, Wasdale Head

If there is one place you should stay in Cumbria for walks to Scafell and around Wasdale and Eskdale, it's the Wasdale Head Inn. It was here that British climbing was born, and the inn celebrates this triumphantly.

As you walk in, boots and poles litter the entrance hall floor, while ice picks and climbing kit of yesteryear decorate the walls. But it is the singular collection of original Abrahams Brothers photographs that mark this place out as a Mecca for climbers – try to spot the manipulated images. The Wasdale Head Inn has six double rooms, three single, one twin and one three-bedded room. With

the exception of one ground floor double room with a four poster bed, all are on the first floor. One of the self-catering apartments has now been created into a family suite and is available to let on a nightly basis. It has two bedrooms to sleep four, but an extra bed can be provided on request.

Food is available from the Abrahams Restaurant, which offers a fine range of locally sourced meals. Hearty pub grub is also available from the bar. A number of real ales are available, including several from the Wasdale Head's own brewery – we recommend the Great Gable.

For more information call 01946 726229 or visit www.wasdale.com

Borrowdale Gates Hotel, Grange

A country house hotel with panoramic views of the Borrowdale valley and the surrounding Lake District fells, including Skiddaw to the north. Situated in two acres of wooded gardens on the edge of the ancient hamlet of Grange, near Keswick, this imposing Lakeland house is set amid the breathtaking scenery of the Borrowdale Valley and close to the shores of Derwent Water, often referred to as the 'Queen of the English Lakes'.

The start of many routes to the summit of Skiddaw can be found just the other side of Keswick, but the hotel is ideally situated for all Lakeland walking, climbing, and touring.

For more information call 01768 777204 or visitwww.borrowdale-gates.com

Pudding Cottage, Ambleside

Lake Lovers has self-catering properties throughout the region. Pudding Cottage, a converted former 18th-century coach house and stables near Ambleside, sleeps six in spacious and luxurious surroundings, all within easy reach of Grasmere, Langdale, Helvellyn and all the great walking associated. Free membership to a health club for the duration of your stay is also included.

For more details call 01539 488855 or visit www.lakelovers.co.uk

King's Head, Thirlspot

A former 17th-century coaching inn situated at the western foot of Helvellyn, with views toward St John in the Vale, Blencathra and Skiddaw. Whether you want to stay here or simply stop for a feed before or after your climb to the top of Helvellyn, there is award-winning food on offer served in two restaurants – the St John restaurant and an a la carte restaurant at the bar – plus plenty of real ales and fine wines.

For those who wish to bed down, the King's Head offers 17 bedrooms, comprising eight doubles (including one four-poster), four twins, two family and three single rooms, all furnished with en suite bathroom, TV and telephone.

For more details call 01768 772393 or visit www.lakedistrictinns.co.uk/KingsHead.

More information

Lake District National Park
Call 01539 724555 or visit
www.lake-district.gov.uk

Cumbria Tourism
www.cumbria-the-lake-district.co.uk
www.golakes.co.uk
www.lakedistrictoutdoors.co.uk

Weatherline *01768 775757*

Spring into action

A few days of wild striding in Northumberland will spring clean your senses and provide a timely reminder of why you love walking so much.

Pictures: **Matthew Roberts**

'**Northumberland** has long been a prize worth fighting for. Centuries of fierce battles and bitter feuds raged over precious pockets of land, the promised loot of barren fells enough to risk spilt blood. The Romans, Danes, Normans and Scots, not to mention dozens of local lawless clans, were all prepared to struggle to the death to get their hands on a slice of this remote borderland.

Strange, then, that Northumberland now lays forgotten by most. Its population density is among the lowest and its national park the least visited in Britain. Look at us walkers – many of us refuse to venture further north than the Lakes, or barely give those once-treasured hills a glance on our way to the loftier peaks of Scotland.

With so few people to absorb its character, Northumberland has become an undiluted assault on the senses. The taste of salty air, the sight of a distant ruin, the touch of an ancient rock carving, the sound of wind racing over heather moors and the smell of butter melting atop enormous teacakes – that's what walking here is all about. It's a grand way to shake off winter and have the reasons you love walking slap you hard in the face.

But don't walk Hadrian's Wall, tread the Pennine Way over the Cheviots or stride any other well-trodden cliché. You can do much, much better than that. Just follow our guide to the finest spots in Northumberland and we guarantee you'll return refreshed and raring to go…

Looking to Bamburgh Castle across Ros Back Sands – enough to get your heart beating, even without a game of 'run from the waves!'

Ross Back Sands

Your footprints are likely to be the only ones on the four-mile-long shore of deserted Ross Back Sands.

> "Ross Back Sands is just the place to vent whatever emotion you have too much of."

"Aeiooooooooo!" It's not a noise I recognise, even though it's screaming from my own mouth. I like to think I'm exhaling the remnants of a winter's worth of stress, rather than losing my marbles – but you decide for yourself. I'm yelling because I can. Because I want to. And because, apart from my walking pal Sarah, there's no one to hear me howl for four miles of sandblasted shoreline.

Ross Back Sands is just the place to vent whatever emotion you have too much of. The wind seems to batter it out of you. This beach is always deserted – the mile-long access walk over turfed sand and through bleached lions' manes of marram grass keeps the type of tourist reliant on public toilets away. And it's always breezy. Somewhat surprising, then, that this has become an unofficial nudist beach, although I've never seen any exposed muscles on my walks here – other than the mussels swept in by the sea, I suppose.

I decide to mark the start of spring with a paddle. Freed from winter-weight socks and boots, my feet appear frighteningly white. But the feeling of sand squelching between my toes brings an involuntary smile. Summer will soon be here.

I cast a satisfying glance to the boundaries of this curling bay, marked to the north by Lindisfarne Castle and to the south by Bamburgh Castle. Far out in the slate-grey sea, the Farne Islands lighthouse flashes a hypnotic greeting. Bliss, if a trifle icy on the toes.

Returning from a walk on Ross Back Sands with ruddy cheeks and bramble hedge hairstyles, there is only one place with teacakes big enough to satisfy our appetites.

The Copper Kettle Tea Rooms are a short drive away in Bamburgh, once the capital of Northumbria and now the decent sort of village that sports a WI noticeboard.

A member of the Tea Council Guild of Tea Shops, it offers shelter and sustenance in an 18th-century parlour and cottage patio garden. I heartily recommend the tipsy tart.

The Route

Route: *Take the lane that leads east between Elwick and Easington Grange Mill towards Ross. Park before you reach Kirkley Hill (grid ref NU132370) and continue on foot to the beach. There are miles of shore to explore, but we suggest you head north-west towards Ross Point for commanding views of Lindisfarne.*

Distance: *It's a 3km return walk to the beach – you can choose how far you follow the shore from there.*

Maps: *Ordnance Survey Explorer 340 or Landranger 75.*

Dunstanburgh Castle

These stark ruins were dubbed romantic in the Victorian age, but I warrant they'll have the hairs on the back of your neck standing to attention.

The castle stands atop basalt cliffs, leaning towers blunt against the darkening sky. They radiate a brooding sense of history as we approach from the north. It's said that the anguished cries of a long-dead knight can still be heard here at midnight, but I reckon it's more likely the cliff's high-rise stack of seabirds that do the squawking.

These ruins need no ghost to add to the atmosphere.

Don't get me wrong – this is a fabulous, rather than a forlorn, place to walk. Crossing Embleton Bay we spot porpoises beating the hardy (or should I say foolhardy?) surfers at their own game. Wrist-thick trunks of seaweed litter the beach and four-foot waves explode on to globate boulders, stacked high on the shore by a pitiless sea.

But it's a deserted, desolate spot. The nearest road is three-quarters of a mile away, so there are no coaches full of denimed day-trippers cluttering the scene, hoping for a quick masterpiece to add to been-there-done-that photo albums. Apart from the odd golfer on the nearby green, there's nothing to remind you that this is the 21st century.

Just the alluring ruin, a rip-roaring swell and more than enough briny air to rouse senses, dulled by a season's central heating, into overdrive. Licking lips that are sapid with salt, we venture closer to the castle.

Built between 1313 and 1315 by Thomas, Earl of Lancaster and High Steward of England, the ruins span an impressive 10 acres of defensible enclosure. Poor Thomas never got to live it up in his new pad – just seven years, after its completion, Edward II had him executed for treason. But the castle has seen its fair share of skirmishes, changing hands five times during the Wars of the Roses.

And, perhaps, that's why neither Sarah nor I have the remotest compulsion to enter the grounds. It's odd, especially when we've walked so far to see the castle at close quarters. But ghosts, battle and bloodshed aren't quite our scene. We choose a rock each and sit down to eat our lunch, scanning the sea for another glimpse of cetacean fin with the finest view in Northumberland behind us.

The Route

Route: Park at the Club House above Embleton Bay (grid ref NU239231) and follow the footpath between the beach and the golf course to Dunstanburgh Castle. Continue south along the coastal path to Craster harbour and turn inland past The Heughs to Dunstan Square, where a bridleway leads north west to Dunstan Steads. Walk into Embleton village, before taking the footpath to Newton Pool Reserve, and return to the car park on the coastal path. For details of opening times and entry prices to Dunstanburgh Castle, call 01665 576231.
Distance: 12km/71/2 miles.
Maps: Ordnance Survey Explorer 332 or Landranger 75.

Put yourself at the mercy of the sea (and errant ghosts) at the most dramatic castle in Northumberland

Beach Court B&B

I'm awakened early by the sounds and smells of the sea wafting through my open bedroom window. Comfy bed or not, I can't resist an early-morning wander, with the National Trust-owned beach not 10 strides from the garden gate.

The tide is freshly out and there are plenty of spoils to be found on the sand, rippled into stripes by the retreating sea. Within a few minutes, my lifetime of shell and odd-shaped pebble beachcombing booty is eclipsed by the discovery of a seal which, sadly, must have died during last night's storm.

The level of in-your-face nature here is intoxicating. But, looking back towards the turreted house where my lavish breakfast awaits, I'm glad that we've found a warm, welcoming enclave to escape its wilder moments.

Stay here

Beach Court is on Harbour Road, Beadnell. For details of accommodation, including the turreted bedroom, call Carole and Russ Field on 01665 720225 or visit www.beachcourt.com

The Route

Route: *From Fenwick (grid ref NU066400), follow St Cuthbert's Way to St Cuthbert's Cave (grid ref NY059352). Take the bridleway leading north west to Holburn, then walk north past Rabbit Hill and through Shiellow Wood to rejoin St Cuthbert's Way.*
Distance: *13.5km/8 1/2 miles.*
Maps: *Ordnance Survey Explorer 340 or Landranger 75.*

St Cuthbert's Cave

Listen to legend and you'll learn that St Cuthbert was no ordinary fellow. The prior of Lindisfarne around 660AD, he became famous for his healing powers. And this was no fickle faculty – when his coffin was prised open 11 years after his death, his body was found perfectly preserved, and enduring fame ensued.

Such was the tale that persuaded Sarah and I to venture up the contours from Fenwick to St Cuthbert's Cave. The link between the marinated saint and the rocky overhang is, admittedly, tenuous – during Viking raids, the saint's relics were carried to safety by the island community, supposedly resting in this cave on the route. But the walk to it is a leafy pleasure through woodland – a scarce commodity in this open countryside – and the views worthy of sainthood.

Below: Walking to St. Cuthbert's cave

Ros Castle

The Route

Route: *From Old Bewick (grid ref NU066215) walk north east to Blawearie, then skirt Hepburn Wood to ascend Ros Castle (grid ref NU081253). Follow the secondary road east, then take the bridleway south west to Tick Law and return to Old Bewick.*
Distance: *16km/10 miles.*
Maps: *Ordnance Survey Explorers 340 and 332 or Landranger 75.*

There is no castle to be seen here – but the finest views of the Cheviots to be had in Northumberland more than compensate.

Sarah and I start our walk deep in the valley below, leaving the River Breamish to climb on to Hepburn Moor, past pine trees contorted into distinctly unconiferous shapes by the relentless wind.

We try hard not to look behind us as we climb, wanting to save the view for the top. Instead, we watch our feet – which is just as well, because the deep ruts of the cart track we're following are filled with rust-hued water, and decaying leaves lurk in the depths like monsters waiting to swallow misplaced boots.

Ros Castle comes into view as we rise above Hepburn Wood. From the flanks of heather-covered moorland, a set of bracken-clad ribs rises to a perfect breast of a hill. This is Ros Castle. The incredible symmetry of its architecture may be all

Mother Nature's work. Or, as an Iron Age hillfort once stood on its summit, I suspect it was human sweat and prehistoric tools that smoothed its contours.

Whatever, it's a grand viewpoint and you will want to linger here. To the west, the whale-backed forms of the Cheviots loom, their tops camouflaged in cloud. It's perplexing to picture them as a volcano 400 million years ago, yet it was the magma spewed from its mouth that formed the tough granite-slabbed crowns that the heather clings to today.

To the east, the coastline basks in sunshine and we can pick out not just the larger Farne Islands, but also the tiny rock-blocks of Megstone and Crumstone. The line of the hill's drystone wall leads my eye towards Holy Island, beckoning us to walk towards its shores. But no, I can see the sparkle of sun on car bonnets there – we have less crowded spots yet to explore.

Black Middens Bastle

"The deep ruts of the cart track we're following are filled with rust-hued water, and decaying leaves lurk in the depths like monsters waiting to swallow misplaced boots."

Treachery and murder was the way of life in 16th-century Northumberland. Families took advantage of the lawless times to pillage, steal and be generally less than neighbourly, and a survey of the time noted that the area was 'plenished with...wild and misdemeaned people'. The only way to survive was to build a defensible farmhouse, known as a bastle, to protect you and yours from marauding raids.

The locals are a lot friendlier these days. But even so, thanks to the solid, four-feet-thick walls, the ruined bastles still stand on the now-quiet fells. Black Middens is one of the area's most interesting and evocative. The steps to its upper-storey entrance are made for much smaller feet than mine and have worn to droopy hollows over the years. Inside, my fingertips explore the weathered half-trunk supports for a long-fallen roof and the windowsills, smoothed to a shine.

English Heritage holds the deeds now, but I wonder what happened to the original occupants who holed up here. Were they killed, or were they murderers themselves? It's an eerie note on which to start our moorland walk.

The Route

Route: *The Reivers Trail follows a waymarked, circular route to a line of ruined bastles, starting at Black Middens (grid ref NY774900).*
Distance: *5km/3 miles.*
Maps: *Ordnance Survey Outdoor Leisure 42 or Landranger 80.*

College Valley

"A blessed lack of people and a lasting reminder of what I love most about walking."

Sat on the slope of an incredible hulk of a hill, I can almost taste the heady sense of freedom. The only speck of man-made pigment in our panorama is our car, abandoned way down below and barely visible through the oncoming rain squalls. Sarah and I have been walking for only an hour, yet it feels like we're deep in the wild brown yonder.

Is there such a place? If, like me, you've spent much of the winter on well-trodden trails within 20 miles of home, you'll be heartened to hear there is – the upper College Valley. The lane leading into this gully is privately owned, and just a dozen cars are allowed to negotiate its potholes each day. But secure a permit and you'll have acres of unpopulated countryside pretty much all to yourself.

As we'd driven over the succession of wooden bridges, climbing steadily upwards, I'd looked for signs of civilisation. I counted just four farmhouses, one church and one heavily-fleeced man. There's a veritable brouhaha of birds – winchats, ring ousels and redstarts will soon be here – and stacks of archaeological remains. Just a blessed lack of people and a lasting reminder of what I love most about walking.

The Route

Route: *There are many circular walking opportunities here, all equally good. To take your car past Hethpool (grid ref NT895284) and into the College Valley you will need a permit. These are free and can be obtained from Sale and Partner Estate Agents, 18-20 Glendale Road, Wooler.*
Map: *Ordnance Survey Landranger 74.*

Lordenshaw

I'm tracing the outline of an indent carved into rock more than 5,000 years ago. Did the hand that fashioned these circular impressions look much like mine? Or was it a thicker-set mitt that clutched a stone or flint between grimy fingers? Whoever that hand belonged to, they've left a more permanent mark on the landscape than I ever will.

Northumberland has many of these cup-and-ring carvings – look on the map and you'll spot a litter of them marked throughout the county – and there are many unfounded theories that attempt to explain their presence. But the truth is that no one really knows what they mean.

Lordenshaw is one of the finest examples to be found. Standing here, the theory mooted that the carving represents a map of nearby hillforts sounds the most feasible to me. There is a hillfort to the east, just one of the 600 identified in the 400 square miles of national park, and it seems logical that its inhabitants would need to know where other settlements lay.

I lean on the rock to scan the patchwork of moorland in front of me, the remains of an old field boundary leading my eye north west to the River Coquet and the Cheviots. I can understand why 19th-century historian Trevelyan tagged Northumberland the land of the far horizon.

But this isn't the weather to stand and stare, and the moisture-sodden winds drive Sarah and I to explore this open access area. There are burial mounds and stone cists, or coffins, to be found here. But it's the bleached bird skull I inadvertently step on that sends a shudder down my spine. This is a wild, bygone landscape that I know nothing about. I know how to clean the spark plugs on my car when it won't start in the morning, what to do when my computer crashes and even (admittedly this has taken me an eon to master) how to set the video. But I doubt I know enough basic life skills to survive long here, even in all my Gore-Tex gear.

But I certainly feel incredibly alive as we head back to Rothbury into the biting wind, in search of tea and solace.

Swallow Fish

Before you leave these untamed parts, pay a visit to the harbour town of Seahouses for the best Northumbrian souvenir money can buy. Hidden away in a maze of back alleys, follow your nose and you will find Swallow Fish, where sea creatures galore are on sale. The crates of giant crabs and kippers are brought from the harbour each morning, ensuring your oceanic feast is as fresh as fresh can be. It's one last treat for your senses to savour.

Shop here: Swallow Fish is hidden away at 2 South Street, Seahouses. For more information call 01665 721052 or visit www.swallowfish.co.uk

Above: Cup and Ring carvings

Before you go...

Further information

For more information on Northumberland National Park *call the park centres at Once Brewed (01434 344396), Rothbury (01669 620887) or Ingram (01665 578248), or visit www.nnpa.org.uk*

The principal tourist information centres *are in Alnwick (01665 510665), Berwick-upon-Tweed (01289 330733), Hexham (01434 652220) and Morpeth (01670 511323).*

For on-line information *visit www.northumbria-tourist-board.org.uk, www.secretkingdom.com and www.northumberland.gov.uk/vg*

The Route

Route: *From Rothbury (grid ref NU057015), walk to Whitton and follow the bridleway along Hillhead Road. Take the footpath leading south past Whittondean to the area of access land above Lordenshaw car park (grid ref NZ053993). Return to Rothbury via the footpath over Garleigh Moor or, for a longer walk, cross the secondary road to follow the permissive path west to Simonside (grid ref NZ024986). Drop through woodland to Great Tosson to follow Carterside Road back to Rothbury.*
Distance: *6km/33/4 miles or 13km/8 miles.*
Maps: *Ordnance Survey Outdoor Leisure 42 or Landranger 81.*

Hadrian's Wall

The brand new Hadrian's Wall National Trail, enchanting Kielder Forest, six all-new heritage paths to Cheviot hillforts, and 'the best place to live in Britain', inland Northumberland awaits

Words: **Perry Cleveland-Peck and Jonathan Manning** Pictures: **Matthew Roberts**

Of all the counties in England, Northumberland is perhaps most associated with wilderness. Its national park is the least populated and most remote – many of us know it only as that rugged bit at the top of the A1 that we look out on as we drive to Scotland. The area's starkness is as much to do with its landscape as its bad luck in being caught in the middle of other people's disagreements.

The Border hills have long been considered a no-go area. The Romans were so frustrated with the recalcitrance of the population to the north, they built a coast-to-coast wall to mark the frontier of its Empire. Later, both William the Conqueror and Edward I wasted armies trying to civilise the locals and to this day, when the Ministry of Defence needs somewhere to practise its warfare or try out a new tank, it knows exactly where to head.

But from the shadow of all this conflict comes a walking heaven. Because agriculture was such a dubious enterprise in Northumbria's yesteryear, most of the uplands that had been settled in prehistoric times were abandoned for the better part of 2,000 years. Which means you can still ramble over the ridges of Steel Rigg in the footsteps of the Emperor Hadrian himself, or walk in the Cheviot hills and stumble upon the untouched remains of Iron Age hillforts established by the 'barbarians' that the Romans were so keen to keep out. Relax in the shade of riverside woodlands untouched for 400 years, or walk through historic Alnwick with its fabulous new gardens, overseen by the forbidding wrought-iron figures guarding the battlements of Alnwick Castle.

Hadrian's Wall

Walk in the footsteps of the second-century Roman legionnaires.

In Monty Python's Life Of Brian, rebellious Reg from the People's Front of Judea asks, "What have the Romans ever done for us?" And while his PFJ pals list 'the sanitation, medicine, education, wine, public order, irrigation, roads, the fresh water system and public health', it is apparent that not one of them is a lover of the country walk. Because the Romans have left us British walkers with one enduring legacy. And now, 2,000 years later, it has just got better.

It took the Romans just 12 years to build Hadrian's Wall, the 12ft high, 73-mile barrier that runs between Bowness on the Solway Firth in the west, to Wallsend on the River Tyne in the east. Given the construction equipment of the time, it was an astonishing achievement, made more so when you consider that the very up-to-date Countryside Agency has just spent more than eight years putting together the footpath that runs alongside it.

But (drum role, please) the Hadrian's Wall National Trail opened May 23rd 2003 and for the first time since the Romans you can now walk the entire length of the wall. The £6 million trail offers walkers the opportunity of stepping back in time with the second-century legionnaires. But its strength is that, while its history sits firmly on Roman foundations, many of the stories it has to tell concern people and events subsequent to the wall's construction, from the seventh-century Dark Age Battle of Heavenfield to General Wade and the 17th-century Jacobite uprising. Like the stones in the wall itself, courses of history sit on top of each other, creating an edifice of times past.

"There is much more to the wall than bricks and mortar," says David McGlade, the Countryside Agency officer responsible for the trail, as we ascend the steep grassy climb to Walltown Crags, a great sinuous spine in the landscape like the vertebrae of some vast diving whale. "There are earthworks everywhere – the North Ditch, which runs much of the length of the wall, the vallum, another trench this time to the south – no one really knows its purpose – buildings, turrets. Virtually every hump in a field and every ridge in the landscape has a tale to tell."

To describe the trail as a single walk doesn't quite do it justice. Yes, there is a new 84-mile national trail running the length of the wall, but, cleverly, David has also created a series of 40 circular walks that take in sections of Hadrian's Wall before darting off through the countryside around it. It is an ingenious method of keeping the erosion down near the precious wall itself, as well as providing some great routes for walkers in varying landscapes. Today, David is guiding us around the Walltown circular, which overlooks 14th-century Thirlwall Castle, built with stones taken from the wall itself.

Hadrian's Wall snakes and stretches away to the distance, even now a bold statement on the earth, as much a psychological barrier as a physical border. On the

> "Like the stones in the wall itself, courses of history sit on top of each other, creating an edifice of times past."

Above: The faint remains of a swastika, carved into the wall almost 2,000 years ago.

The Route

Walltown Circular

Distance: 11km/63/4 miles
Route: From Walltown Quarry (grid ref NY669660) head west to Thirlwall Castle then north to Wood House. Pick up footpath heading south west then, from grid ref NY654666, go north west to Wardrew Wood. Head south along River Irthing to Gisland and follow Hadrian's Wall National Trail east to quarry car park.

David is immensely proud of what he and his team have accomplished, but he concedes that the Roman achievement is by far the more impressive. "I admire them for their organisation," he says. "To quarry tens of thousands of blocks of stone, to dress the blocks, to take them to site, to build the limestone kilns for the mortar, all this took immense organisation. I wonder what they would think of us today."

The wall here on the crags is at its tallest, some seven or eight feet high. But along the length of the trail it is not always the case. In places, the wall has disappeared from sight, plundered over time and used in the construction of later buildings and trackways. But evidence of its creators is never too far away. "The archaeology is just centimetres underfoot," says David, "and it is important to remember this." He is only too aware of the impact walkers can have on this World Heritage Site, and

has done his very best to protect it. Flagstones are placed along potential soggy stretches of the trail and around gateways where boots can wear away the soil. Hidden people counters have been positioned en route to monitor the passage of visitors. And a regular photographic survey, analysed together with rainfall data from the Met Office, will provide vital information on how the trail is bearing up under the strain.

The result is a walk celebrating 2,000 years that uses the latest know-how to bring it to life. If we treat it carefully, it should last for another two millennia.

northern side of the wall, a sharp rocky drop of 50m or so – no need for the North Ditch here – and the rolling farming land of Hangingshield Rigg, where once barbarians roamed. To the south, 'civilisation' – General Wade's military road stretches east-west, parallel to the wall here, in places running directly on top of it (in a startling act of official vandalism, Wade's troops used parts of the wall as foundations for what is now the B6318). Further south, an undulating earthy patchwork of yellow-brown fields and leafy woodlands, winking in turn as the evening clouds pass overhead. From the fields below, the shrill call of a kestrel hangs upon the witching-hour breeze.

We stop for a moment and David points out an inverted swastika, carved into the ancient blocks as a good luck talisman by some lonely sentry two millennia ago, perhaps thinking of home on the Med, or further afield in Africa maybe – it comes as some surprise to learn that there were black faces among the wall's Roman builders.

Hadrian's Wall facts

"Hadrian was the first to build a wall, 80 miles long, to separate the Romans and the barbarians" – Roman biography of Hadrian.

Hadrian's Wall was started in 122AD and took 12 years to complete. It is the most important monument built by the Romans in Britain.

At its height, the Roman Empire stretched from Britain to present-day Iraq and southwards to the Sahara. For 300 years, Hadrian's Wall was the Roman Empire's north-east frontier.

Hadrian's Wall was not an impenetrable barrier – think of it as a border crossing. At mile intervals there were gates, each defended by a guard post known as a 'milecastle'. Two towers or turrets were placed between each milecastle.

In front of the wall was a ditch, except where the crags made it superfluous, with the material from the ditch placed on the northern side to form a mound.

Behind the wall a 'vallum' was constructed, an earthwork running the length of the frontier. Between the wall and the vallum was a road.

The construction of the wall was carried out almost exclusively by soldiers from the three legions of the province: The Second, based near Newport, Wales; the Sixth from York; and the Twentieth from Chester. Most of the soldiers stationed on the wall were British. Slaves were not used on the wall.

The best places to see the wall are at Wallsend, Sewingshields to Steel Rigg, Cawfields, Walltown Crags and from Gisland to Birdoswald.

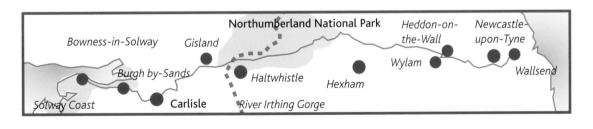

Hadrian's Wall Path

Kielder Forest

Enchanting walks in a man-made environment

If the ancients made their mark on the Northumberland landscape, so have we. And no more so than at Kielder Forest where one of the largest lakes was built in 1982, capable of holding a staggering 200,000 million litres of water.

Around this vast lake is Britain's biggest forest, covering more than 600 square kilometres. The forest is a major timber producer, but it is sustainable and diverse. Timber is harvested at the same rate that the forest is growing, and broad-leaf trees are planted alongside conifers to break up the uniform nature and age of the woodlands.

The lake and the forest make for some exhilarating low-level walking. In today's spring sunshine the area takes on an invigorating, almost Alpine feel. And the authorities responsible for the area – Northumbrian Water and the Forestry Commission – have teamed up to provide some truly outstanding trails, not to mention a number of man-made distractions to make a day's walking in the area a memorable experience.

A ferry operates on the lake in the summer, and walkers can use this service to travel to key locations around the 27-mile shoreline – get dropped off here, take a walk through the woods there, head for another jetty and cruise to more walking locations further up the lake. It makes for a pleasant and diverting means of trekking the choice bits of this huge forest.

Today, the Forestry Commission's Pippa Kirkham has joined us, promising a couple of great walks and, intriguingly, a few 'surprises'. We're on the Duchess Trail, a genteel two-miler around Kielder Castle on the northern shore of the water, the great forest rising up to the skies on all sides. "It is an absolute wilderness," says Pippa with a sweep of her hand. "It's the scale that is so impressive, like standing on a beach looking at the ocean or the stars at night. It puts you – everything – into perspective. There aren't many places like it left in the country."

Back at the castle and it's time for one of Pippa's surprises. "The Kielder landscape is home to a hidden collection of interactive sculptures," she says. "Artists and architects have created a number of installations here inspired by the area's vastness and beauty. They have been placed in secret areas around the lake."

Our second walk of the day starts at Plashetts Jetty, one of the ferry stops on Kielder Water. Once upon a time, the incline here was home to a village and a railway line that carried trolleys from Plashetts colliery to a freight depot on the now submerged Border Counties railway line, a watery ghost train many metres below the surface of the lake.

> "The Wave Chamber sits on the shore as if it were built here at the birth of time – it's a magical way to end a magical walk."

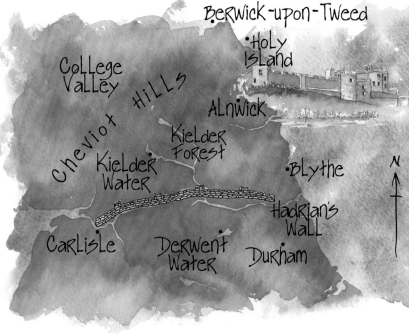

The Route

Wave Chamber Walk
Distance: 8.4km/5¼ miles)
Route: *Catch ferry to Plashetts Jetty (grid ref NY674901). Head south along shore path then east to Benny Shank for second jetty (NY685885). Cruise to Belling Crags (NY694886) and walk around crags for sculpture (NY696882). Head east, then south across dam, then west to Tower Knowe for ferry.*

We head south, hugging the rocky shoreline, the sun on our faces, a spring in our crunching steps. On our left are the remains of an ancient deer park, part of a walled estate near Mounces that once enclosed this part of the valley. South still, and Pippa points out the site of Plashetts Quarry, which sits on the line of the Whin Sill, the volcanic dolomite that extends across Northumberland from the Farne Islands all the way to Crag Lough on Hadrian's Wall.

At Benny Shank we come across a most odd construction. The Belvedere, created by Softroom architects, is an award-winning walkers' shelter, clad on the outside in eye-watering reflective metal. It's shape seems to pull in and reflect the liquid panoramas around it – a giant kaleidoscope twisting the lakescape. Inside, the gold lining and yellow skylight provide a soft and warm space for walkers to sit until the ferry arrives. As we wait for ours, Pippa points out another beguiling shape on the horizon that looks like a giant beehive floating on the water. "That's where you're heading," she says.

Our ferry arrives, Pippa departs and after a short boat ride we're on terra firma at The Belling – but for a thin promontory, an island adrift on Kielder Water. We follow the shoreline around the island, at once climbing through the tall larch trees, then tumbling down past great slabs of rock hanging above the water. Our path twists ahead of us, the 'surprise' just around every corner.

Then we are upon it. The Wave Chamber is a large, stone, conical structure built by artist Chris Dury out of 81 tonnes of local rock. In contrast to the Belvedere, it sits on the shore as if it were built here at the birth of time.

The object is a camera obscura, designed to reflect an image from the outside on to a screen inside. We step through the small door and let our eyes become accustomed to the dark. Then the floor seems to come alive. Ripples from the lake outside are projected on to it and dance across the circular base, the sunlight sparking between our feet. For a moment we're walking on water, dizzy with the unreal situation.

Walking on water – it's a magical way to end a magical walk.

Top: The award-winning Belvedere, Kielder's kaleidoscopic walkers' shelter.

Middle: A surprise around every corner as the path twists ahead.

Bottom: The 16th-century packhorse bridge on the moss and fern clad Duchess Trail near Kielder Castle.

Cheviot Hills

Walk the College Valley's hillfort heritage trails.

Hadrian's Wall is a demonstration of imperial power. How else can you explain a barrier that cleaves an island in two? But as you walk it, you can't help glancing north and wondering just who these so-called 'barbarians' were that Hadrian and his Roman Empire were so anxious to keep out.

Beneath the mighty Cheviot mountain on the England-Scotland border, north of the wall, lies College Valley, an isolated, burn-splashed basin graced by tumbling waterfalls, breathtaking hills and a wind fierce enough to tear the words straight from your mouth.

Upon these rugged hills lies evidence of human activity from the late Stone Age onwards. Most impressive is the spectacular concentration of mysterious Iron Age hillforts, older even than Hadrian's Wall. The hardy people who lived here were the ancestors of those who so troubled Hadrian. And for the first time in history, us walkers have the opportunity to step into their world.

Iain Hedley, an archaeologist with the Northumberland National Park, has spent £1 million to construct a series of waymarked heritage trails to these hillforts. Much of the trails run across private land and access has only recently been granted. Whether you're interested in our islands' history or not, the trails offer some truly outstanding, first-class walking.

Today, Ron, Gareth and Bobby from the Northumberland Long Distance Walkers' Association, Kim from the national park and Iain have joined us for an exclusive walk to a number of the hillforts – what Iain calls his 'Ring Chesters Round'.

"The first myth to dispel concerns the term 'hillfort'," says Iain, as he leads our party from the car park at Hethpool on to the flanks of White Hill. "In the 19th century, antiquaries thought the ancient Britons were bloodthirsty barbarians living in a society based on hostile, marauding tribes. They decided these structures were defensive. Now we're less convinced this is the case."

We climb in a series of steps. Ancient cultivation terraces still mark the hill's flanks, going back at least as far as the Iron Age. They provide flats for welcoming breathers on our ascent to the top. To our

The Route

Ring Chesters Round
Distance: 9km/5½ miles
Route: *From car park (grid ref NT894281) head north along road to footpath on White Hill for hillfort on East Laddies Knowe. Head north west across Black Bog to quarry (NT873292), then south west to plantation and follow path through to Ring Chesters. Head south west, then south east, and pick up St Cuthbert's Way back to car park.*
To combine this walk with another hillfort trail , try Iain's Hetha's Hike (4km/2½ miles) by picking up footpath at grid ref NT883282 for the Little Hetha and a (steep) climb to Great Hetha hillforts, before heading south east for footpath, then north along a track to the car park.

right, halfway up, are the remains of an ancient burial mound, two standing stones that to this day offer spiritual solace at times of loss to locals on the estate.

We head across the top of a small plantation to East Laddies Knowe, the first of the hillforts on our journey today. On the ground the fort is difficult to see – the earth rather than stone ramparts are more discernable from the air. But Iain points out a circular dip underfoot, evidence of a later enclosure built on the foundations of the first.

"Modern archaeologists believe that the Iron Age communities were relatively peaceful," says Iain. "Far from being defensive, there is a certain 'impressing the neighbours' element to some of the forts."

He points north. "A good example of this is at Staw Hill, just over there. The section of wall facing the neighbouring hillfort on Mid Hill was large and elaborate, whereas on the opposite side the ramparts are lower and more simple in construction."

We head north across the stile at Black Bogs and stop for a well-earned coffee break at a disused quarry, the rock face providing an agreeable shelter from the stiff north-easterly wind.

Flasked up, we dip south west into the plantation

Iron Age hillforts are scattered across the Cheviot Hills. At first glance they can be tricky to see, but from the air (right) their circular constructions can clearly be seen.

"For some reason this really touches me – to share the hearth of our most ancient ancestors seems the most intimate of connections."

at Haddon Hill, a diverting conifer wood that offers some shade from the spring sun that cuts through the hilltop wind. The tracks here are occasionally used by the local hunt and, today, the going is uneven and difficult.

A short, steep climb on the other side brings us to Ring Chesters, the most impressive of the ancient sites on our walk today. Two crumbling drystone ramparts protect the windswept inner circle, in which the remains of later circular buildings are visible. Inside one there is a small collection of stones piled in a circle. "The fireplace," Iain informs us, "around which our ancient forefathers warmed and fed themselves. For some reason this really touches me – to share the hearth of our most ancient ancestors seems the most intimate of connections."

Standing here, it's hard to believe that these people really were the barbarians we once thought. The situation of their communities seems very civilised indeed, a hilltop each in a valley so picturesque it makes your heart sing. The only crime we can discern is the fact that it has taken us so long to see it.

Standing stones beneath East Laddies Knowe – to this day they offer spiritual solace to the locals.

The hillfort trail is well sign-posted

Alnwick

The best walks and views in Britain's best place to live.

Above: Seven castles can be seen from Brizlee Tower.

Below: The ruins of Hulne Priory.

The Route

Hulne Park

Route: From Alnwick Castle gatehouse (grid ref NU186136) go up Bailiffgate and straight on into Hulne Park. Follow road and, 180m after Park Farm, go left uphill. Take right fork to Brizlee Tower. Pass tower, follow path and go left at crossroads, passing cave on left. Descend hill and retrace steps.

The medieval inhabitants of Alnwick would never have believed it. This handsome town, besieged over centuries, is now 'officially' the 'best place to live in Britain'.

Its status as preferred Borders battlefield for English and Scots has been transformed by a combination of strong local identity, historic buildings, good local food, affordable housing, low crime rate and decent transport facilities.

The town's only negative score in the 'best place' survey was for its climate, the air chilled by a biting North Sea wind. But an extra layer protects the bones of country walkers from this perishing blast.

Indeed, the best place to view 'the best place to live' is arguably from a windy hill on the immediate outskirts of the town, on a route that starts in Alnwick.

With Alnwick Castle gatehouse behind us, its battlements guarded by fierce wrought-iron warrior figures, we head down Bailiffgate, keeping straight ahead as the B6346 bends to the right. We're heading for Hulne Park, but just before we enter, a discreet monument on our left celebrates the capture of King William the Lion of Scotland on this spot. He was besieging the town in 1174, but suffered a reversal of fortune and was taken prisoner by an English force. Whether coincidence or divine intervention, his capture took place on the day that King Henry II subjected himself to flogging by Canterbury monks, as penance for his role in the death of Thomas à Becket.

The film Becket, starring Richard Burton and Peter O'Toole, was filmed in Hulne Park, whose 3,000 acres of woodland, moorland, crag, riverside and pasture are enclosed by an impossibly grand nine-mile wall.

Following the road and blue waymarks, we turn sharply up White Hill to our left, Alnwick Castle appearing to hover over the woodland behind us with the same airborne magic of Harry Potter's Quidditch match – filmed at the castle. Beyond, the North Sea sparkles on the horizon, while in the valley to our right nestle the well-preserved ruins of Hulne Priory, built by the Carmelites in 1240.

Heading along the River Aln, in the shadows of Alnwick Castle.

"The views from ground level seize the breath as sharply as the climb."

Better panoramas await as the broad track continues to Brizlee Hill and a plateau dominated by Brizlee Tower, a Robert Adam pseudo-Gothic folly dating from 1781. The view from the top covers no fewer than seven castles, including Warkworth to the south and Bamburgh to the north, and although the tower is now closed, the views from ground level seize the breath as sharply as the climb. Yet they are arguably eclipsed by the vista of Northumberland that opens further up the track, where an obelisk and stone bench provide a resting place to admire miles of stunning countryside.

Following the path we stumble across the Cave of the Nine Year Old, guarded by an 18th-century stone figure, part priest, part warrior, before the track leads back to the entrance of the park.

The best place to live in Britain? It's quite a transformation for a town once beset by battles, sieges and skirmishes.

Before you go...

VISIT HERE

Northumberland

Northumberland National Park Authority, *tel: 01434 605555, www.nnpa.org.uk*

Northumbria Tourism,
www.visitnorthumbria.com or call the tourism enquiry line on 0906 683 3000 (calls charged at 25p per minute).

Countryside Agency, *North East, tel: 0191 269 1600.*

Hexham tourist information centre, *tel: 01434 652220.*

Forestry Commission, *Bellingham, tel: 01434 220242.*

Northumberland Wildlife Trust,
tel: 0191 284 6884.

Northumbria Tourist Board,
tel: 0191 375 3000.

Northumberland Long Distance Walkers' Association.
Call Ron Chambers on 01207 563869 or visit www.ldwa.org.uk

Visitor centres:

Once Brewed, *tel: 01434 344396.*

Rothbury, *tel: 01669 260887.*

Ingram, *tel: 01665 578248.*

Please follow the trail's code of conduct.

Hadrian's Wall

For more details on the short circular walks, including individual route descriptions, or for any other details about Hadrian's Wall call:

National Trail Development Officer *on 0191 269 1600.*

Hadrian's Wall Tourism *on 01434 602505.*

Hadrian's Wall Helpline *on 01434 322002.*

David McGlade *has created a passport system for the wall. Walk it entirely and you can collect six passport stamps to prove you are as good as the Romans. There are a number of Roman settlements along the trail, which David and his team positively encourage you to visit. For more information call the following numbers.*

Chester's Roman Fort, *tel: 01434 681379*

Housesteads Roman Fort, *tel: 01434 344363*

Vindolanda, *tel: 01434 344277*

Kielder

Kielder Castle Forest Park Centre, *tel: 01434 250209.*

Leaplish Waterside Park, *tel: 01434 250312.*

Tower Knowe visitor centre, *tel: 01434 240398.*

Forestry Commission, Bellingham, *tel: 01434 220242.*

Kielder Water Cruises, *tel: 01434 250312.*
The 80-seater 'Osprey' runs from March 23rd until October 31st. Osprey has a bar, shop, heated lounge and toilets. It sails four times a day around the lake, calling at Leaplish and Tower Knowe, and requested stops on the north shore. Departure times from Leaplish are 10.15am, 11.35am, 2pm and 3.20pm.

There are 12 pieces of art and architecture hidden at Kielder. For more details visit www.kielder.org

A novel 'rent-a-ranger' scheme has been launched at Kielder Castle. For details call 01434 250209.

Cheviots

For more information on the five new **Hillfort Heritage Trails** *visit www.nnpa.org.uk or call the national park visitor centre on 01668 282406 or 01434 605555.*

Alnwick

Castle open daily until October 31st,

11am-5pm. Alnwick Gardens open all year, 10am-8pm or dusk, if earlier. tel: 01665 510777.

Hulne Park is open 11am to sunset most days. No dogs allowed.

Maps

Ordnance Survey Landrangers 75, 80, 81, 86 and 87; Explorers OL16, 42, 43 and 316.

Harvey Maps Superwalker Cheviot Hills.

STAY HERE

The Pheasant Inn,
Kielder Water,
Hexham,
Northumberland.
Call Mr Kershaw on 01434 240382 or visit www.thepheasantinn.com

Allerwash Farmhouse,
Newbrough,
Hexham,
Northumberland.
Call 01434 674574.

Silverton Lodge, *an award-winning bed and breakfast in Rothbury, on the edge of the national park. Self-catering accommodation is also available. Silverton Lodge, Silverton Lane, Rothbury, Northumberland. Call 01669 620144 or visit info@silvertonlodge.co.uk*

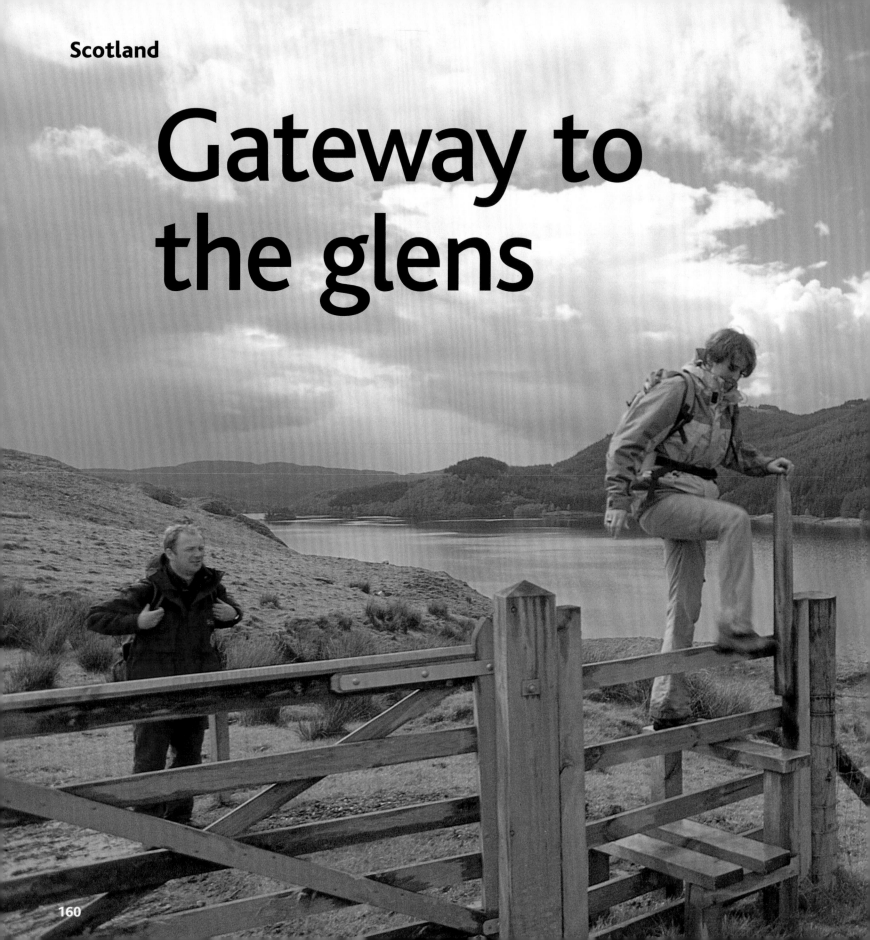

Gateway to the glens

Until a recently, Scotland stood with Iraq and Albania as one of only three countries in the world without a national park. But not any more.

Words: **Emma Kendell** Pictures: **Matthew Roberts**

Conic Hill

Looking west across Loch Lomond from the top of Conic Hill. Not a bad way to work up an appetite for breakfast.

I am standing atop Conic Hill, a gem of a hummock on the south-east shore of Loch Lomond. The waters of the loch are still, the surrounding hills shrouded in cloud. A line of islands in front of me disappears into the mist, their banks densely studded with trees. Aside from the magnolia paint-splats of distant sheep, nothing is moving in the landscape.

> "The waters of the loch are still, the surrounding hills shrouded in cloud. A line of islands in front of me disappears into the mist. This is the best view of the loch I've ever seen."

"This is the best view of the loch I've ever seen," I tell Country Walking's photographer, Matt. "Look at that island down there," I urge him. "Wouldn't you like to live there?" There is no answer. Matt is asleep.

It is seven o'clock in the morning, so I forgive Matt for dozing off. Last night in the pub, this pre-breakfast hill assault seemed like a first-rate idea. Bleary-eyed in the rain at the Balmaha car park an hour ago, where pungent whiffs of wild garlic shook our sleepy senses awake, it all seemed a bit too real.

Following the West Highland Way, we managed the short, sharp climb to the top of Conic Hill in half an hour, albeit with gritted teeth. But the view, hidden from us until we were minutes from the top, temporarily wiped out any weariness. For this cone is a geological pudding mix of sandstone and quartz, standing on the boundary fault between the lowlands and highlands of Scotland. Far to the south lie the dull plains whence we came. But to the north, east and west are the lofty contours of the national park we have yet to explore. Even with the wind buffeting around my head, and my view restricted through the porthole of my hood, I can't help but feel excited.

I lie down in rough grass next to Matt, chancing on a cushion of heather for a pillow, and feel the soft rain on my eyelids. It's a fine start to our grand tour of Loch Lomond and the Trossachs, and we still have a huge, haggis-embellished breakfast to look forward to. Can life get any better?

The Route

Distance: *8km/5 miles.*
Route: *Park in Balmaha car park (grid ref NS421910) and take the West Highland Way leading out of the car park into the forest. Turn left in Balmaha Plantation up a stepped path to reach the summit of Conic Hill (grid ref NS432923). Continue on the West Highland Way to Garadhban Forest, turning right on to a track to Milton of Buchanan.*
Return to Balmaha on the roadside footpath.
Maps: *Ordnance Survey Landrangers 56 and 57 or Outdoor Leisure 39, Harvey Route Map of the West Highland Way.*

Ben More

I'll be honest with you. We didn't make it up this mighty mountain on our grand tour of the national park. On the day we had earmarked for our ascent, Ben More's lower slopes, never mind its summit, were lost in cloud. Save for getting Heather the weather-girl's head on a plate with a dash of ketchup, there wasn't a lot we could do.

But, darn it, I was disappointed. You see, I have a soft spot the size of South America for Ben More. It was my first Munro.

The idea of walking up a Munro (a mountain over 3,000ft) had filled me with fear. But the reality, when I sweated buckets on its contours two summers ago, was far more enjoyable. The mountain was kind to its vertigo-ridden Munro virgin. Aside from one short section, where hands as well as feet were needed, the terrain was good. And the panorama from its 3,851ft pinnacle was more than just reward for the four-hour slog up its pathless flank.

Take it from me – if you are planning to climb just one big hill on your tour, make it Ben More.

The Route

Distance: *Route dependent – but this is steep terrain, so start early and allow a full day for the walk.*
Route: *Park in the car park on the shore of Loch Lubhair (grid ref NN424268). After a short walk along the A85, take the track that leads behind Benmore Farm (signed Ben More). From here it's very much up to you – for the most direct (but also the most difficult) route, head up the north-west slope. Otherwise follow Benmore Burn south, before tracking one of its tributary streams to the saddle between Ben More and Stob Binnein, where you'll find a path leading to the summit (grid ref NN432244). Choose a fine day, pack appropriate clothing and carry (and use!) a map and compass.*
Maps: *Ordnance Survey Landranger 51, Harvey Superwalker Crianlarich.*

Glen Finglas

"Long and winding roaaad..." I can't help but hum the tune to myself, and I'm sure national park ranger Steve Kenney wishes I'd stop. But after a one-and-a-half-mile climb from the village of Brig o' Turk in torrential rain, a miracle has happened. The sun has come out just as we emerge from the silver birch wood that has so far muffled our steps. Ahead, I can see the track twisting past the reservoir and on up an isolated glen dotted with broken bronze stalks of bracken, tempting our strides to quicken. If it wasn't for the company, I'd skip down this track.

It's easy to get carried away by such a place, something that John Ruskin, who stayed here with his wife, Euphemia Gray, and artist friend John Everett Millais in the summer of 1853, learned to his cost. On their painting excursions and walking expeditions around the glen, illicit love flowered between Millais and Euphemia, resulting in the biggest marital scandal to rock fashionable society at that time.

But we are in search of less amorous excitement today. Steve says there's a slim chance of spotting a golden eagle. Our first feathered sighting is none too promising – a pair of mallards on the water – but, the further we walk, the more we can tick off on our mental I-Spy list. Buzzard – tick! Kestrel – tick! Sparrowhawk – tick!

Despite a crick in the neck from our skyward scanning, the box beside eagle remains infuriatingly blank.

But this is a good day's walk. Although it's easy to navigate and the terrain is firm, we will reach the 2,000ft mark and pass through plenty of windswept and wildly beautiful country. Perhaps the eagle will be waiting for us there.

Glen Finglas – enough to make Emma sing Beatles songs.

The Route

Distance: *25km/15 miles.*
Route: *Park by the village hall in Brig o' Turk (grid ref NN535067) and follow the access road north past Glen Finglas Reservoir. Where the track forks below Gread na Croiteige, bear right. Follow the stream of Allt Gleann nam Meann. Stay on this track around the mass of Meall Cala and descend Glen Finglas to the fork, where you retrace your steps back to the village.*
Maps: *Ordnance Survey Landranger 57, Harvey Superwalker Ben Ledi.*

Ben A'an

If you yearn for a mountain-top vista, but your legs won't carry you there, Ben A'an is an excellent alternative to Ben More. It takes just an hour to reach the summit and the views, while less dramatic, are much, much more than you deserve for such a short walk.

The Route

Distance: *3.2km/2 miles.*
Route: *From the car park on the north shore of Loch Achray (grid ref NN509070), follow the well-defined path north north east, and then north west, to Ben A'an (grid ref NN502083). Return by the same route.*
Maps: *Ordnance Survey Landranger 57, Harvey Superwalker Ben Ledi.*

Puck's Glen

"Eeurgghhh." A water droplet big enough to bathe in finds annoyingly accurate aim and dribbles down my spine. My cheeks shine from waterfall spray and my boots squelch through the mulch of last year's soggy pine cones. Puck's Glen is no place to stay dry.

But I really shouldn't moan – it's water that has created this fern-laden, fairytale chasm that is sheer, unadulterated delectation for walkers. From the slopes of Cnoc a'Mhadaidh high above me, an energetic stream the colour of strong espresso has carved this forested glen into pools of cappuccino froth. In the quiet, dank depths that the sunlight rarely reaches, it's this Adam's ale that gives life to greens galore. Mosses mix with wood sorrel and pennywort. Sage-hued lichen makes miniature rainforests out of ancient tree stumps, while ferns unfurl fronds the vibrant shade of gladioli leaves.

Enveloped in this wonderland, I make slow progress up the path that leads from the valley floor, stopping to gaze, gape and gander from each of the narrow wooden footbridges that criss-cross the brook. Squeezing between two boulders, the trail rounds a corner to a tiny grove, where a huge conifer spreads protective branches over a pool at the base of a tiny, tumbling waterfall. It's the sort of spot where undiscovered species lay hidden. Or even trolls. Further on, I find a perfectly formed arch not four inches high among the roots of a tree. Is this the entrance to an elfish underworld?

Perhaps the water has seeped into my brain.

> **"Water has created this fern-laden, fairytale chasm. It's the sort of spot where undiscovered species lay hidden. Or even trolls."**

The Route

Distance: *5.5km/3 1/2 miles. There is a track leading over the saddle between Meall Dubh and Creag Mhòr should you wish to extend the walk.*
Route: *Park in the Forest Enterprise car park off the A815, south of Loch Eck (grid ref NS146839). Walk north along the tarmac track for 350m and turn right into Puck's Glen (grid ref NS147843). At the top of the glen, follow a forestry track, then a path north north west, returning along the tarmac track.*
Maps: *Ordnance Survey Landranger 56.*

Balquhidder

An American tourist is tying a tartan ribbon to the grave of Rob Roy MacGregor. Her husband takes a snap. No doubt the folks back home will be suitably impressed. I'd like a closer look at Rob Roy's sword-inscribed grave, and at the ruins of the 17th-century church, but I can't linger in this well-visited place of pilgrimage.

I follow a path that leads from the far corner of the churchyard, alongside a river crowded with mossy boulders. When the forest of Kirkton Glen spits me out on to wild, uninhabited upland, where cairns and shielings (shelters) are the only landmarks, I'm forced to fish out my map and compass to separate the trail from the sheep paths. Rob Roy would once have walked this way, an ancient path linking Balquhidder with Glen Dochart. Up here, it's easy to imagine illicit 18th-century shenanigans and clashes between warring clans. This is where those tourists should be paying homage to the infamous cattle snaffler.

"You don't need to climb high to enjoy the best views, and this walk proves it. In just four miles I've taken in vistas of Loch Lomond, Ben Lomond and the Arrochar Alps."

Luss

Tucked away in a back street of the conservation village of Luss, I touch a crumbling part of Scotland's history that is 1,000 years old, a legacy of a Viking invasion. It was 1263 when Haakon of Norway passed through the village, after his army had dragged their ships overland from Arrochar to Tarbet, to plunder settlements on the shore of Loch Lomond. But one Viking never left. The poor fellow lies here beneath my feet, under a gravestone intricately carved with tiles and roof supports to resemble a longhouse, and a lasting reminder of home.

Cruach Tairbeirt

Sitting on a convenient bench,

I ponder the view while I wait for my breath to catch up with me. Loch Long lies peacefully below, its torpedo range long since shut. From its shores, I see a beguiling path leading up to the distinctive

Cobbler. You'll most likely find this hunk of a rock marked on maps as Ben Arthur. But it's such a well-known, prominent peak, all know it by its affectionate moniker.

I'd love to include the primary nobble of the Cobbler on our grand tour but, without a few deft climbing moves, we'd never bag its summit safely. I, for one, would be petrified. "You don't need to climb high to enjoy the best views in the park," says ranger Steve Kenney. And this walk along the southern slopes of Cruach Tairbeirt proves it. In the space of four miles I've taken in some of the finest vistas of all that is central to the national park – Loch Lomond, Ben Lomond and the Arrochar Alps. And all without a precipice in sight.

The Route

Distance: *7.3km/4 1/2 miles.*
Route: *Parking in Arrochar is limited – if the main car park is full (grid ref NN296041), try Succoth (grid ref NN296050). The path leads you uphill from the telephone box (grid ref NN298044). Keep right to follow the contours around the hillside to the north east. Where the path forks above the railway station (grid ref NN311047), turn left to follow a circular track which leads you back to the fork. Retrace your steps to Arrochar*
Maps: *Ordnance Survey Outdoor Leisure 39, Harvey Superwalker Arrochar Alps.*

Loch Katrine

The wave-lapped beauty of Loch

Katrine that inspired Sir Walter Scott to pen The Lady of the Lake has also led to its downfall... armies of camera-touting tourists who think walking is something you do between the coach and the tartan-tableclothed teashop. But fear not! Catch the steamer SS Sir Walter Scott (yes, I'm afraid some of those softy sightseers will do the same) to sail to the loch's far side at Stronachlachar and you will soon have the best of Loch Katrine to yourself. Wave a smug goodbye to the foolish masses who paid for a return trip, and feast on the huddle of hills all around you.

The Route

Distance: *19km/12 miles on the loch-side track. Add another 6km/3 3/4 miles to explore Glen Gyle.*
Route: *The steamer leaves from the Trossachs Pier on the eastern tip of Loch Katrine (grid ref NN494073) – for timetables and tariffs call 01877 376316 or visit www.lochkatrine.org.uk – and sails to Stronachlachar (grid ref NN404102). Follow the track clockwise around the loch in search of ancient burial grounds, old clan hideouts and views as far as Ben Ledi. Don't miss a detour up the tangled contours of Glen Gyle.*
Maps: *Ordnance Survey Landrangers 56 and 57, Harvey Superwalker Ben Lomond and Loch Katrine.*

Carrick Castle

The Route

Distance: *13km/8 miles.*
Route: *From the car park by Finart Bay (grid ref NS189885) take the path north from Shepherd's Point. Turn right when this joins a forestry road, and right again to follow a path above Rubha nan Eoin until it joins a tarmac road to Carrick Castle. Return by the same route.*
Maps: *Ordnance Survey Landranger 56.*

There are strange noises at Carrick Castle. A shriek. A squawk. Odd, guttural grunts leading to angry cries. A caterwauling of ungodly proportions. This clamour is all the more startling because it follows a gentle, peaceful wander along the shores of Loch Long and then Loch Goil.

When I'd detoured from the path on to a grassy jut of land to get my first glimpse of this 16th century castle, the three-storey tower had looked an eerily quiet spot. It sits on a rocky promontory of Loch Goil, guarding the wooded slopes all around it with an air of neglected duty, arising from the nettles growing on its window ledges. A forbidding grey Royal Navy ship gliding past only added to the silence.

So what is this commotion? The castle was used as a hunting lodge by the Campbells, and set on fire in 1685 to punish this powerful clan who supported a rebellion against King James VII. Perhaps vengeful spirits still lurk in its mortarless walls?

I creep closer, relieved when my boots reach a sweep of reeds and plantain after crunching noisily across the mussel-strewn shore. And then I see the cause of the hullabaloo. A goose has made her nest at the foot of the tower and, judging by the swear words shrieking from her beak, she doesn't like the look of me.

Rest and be thankful

No visit to these parts is complete without a stop at the Rest and be thankful. Be under no illusions – this grandly named place is just a car park, adorned with a mobile eyesore of a café and frequented by men with mountain goatees. But it's a veritable institution in the outdoors world, high in the hills with a 360-degree panorama of peaks. The hooked summit of the Cobbler stands to the south east, with craggy Beinn an Lochain to the north west. Beinn Luibhean lies to the east, its slopes rutted with rivulets, while the forested flanks of Ben Bonich and the grassy nub of The Brack disappear to the south. After a walk up the steep-sided valley from Ardgartan, never has a view looked, or a gulp of over-brewed tea from a polystyrene cup tasted, so good.

The Route

Distance: *14km/8 3/4 miles.*
Route: *Park in the car park in Ardgartan (grid ref NN269036) and walk north west up Glen Croe to the Rest and be thankful (grid ref NN230073). Return by using the same route.*
Maps: *Ordnance Survey Landranger 56, Harvey Superwalker Arrochar Alps.*

Gleann Auchreoch

The twisting, tangled branches
of this exposed slope have been bonsai-ed by the
constant battle against the elements. From a
distance, the trees take on a bushy, deciduous form.
It's only when I step closer that I realise these are
Scots pines, remnants of the ancient Caledonian
Forest which once carpeted vast tracts of Scotland.

It makes for a fascinating walk. Marked on the
map as coniferous wood, this is the most beautiful
pine forest you will ever have the pleasure of
exploring. I guarantee it. The woodland is open,
leaving the flowing green slopes punctuated with
alpine flowers. Long views of Ben Lui's fearsome
inclines lurch above the treeline. Mounds of glacial
moraine litter the valley, while tadpoles swim in
puddles on the track. This forest may be ancient
but, compared to the deathly quiet of newer, denser
plantations, it is singing with life.

The Route

Distance: *10.5km/6 1/2 miles.*
Route: *Turn off the A82 and park
before you reach the
bridge (grid ref NN345289).
Cross the bridge and turn right.
About 200m after crossing a
railway bridge, turn right on a
path (not marked on some
maps, grid ref NN334283).
Cross a footbridge and turn left
on a clear path. After crossing a
stream, join a forestry road. After
crossing another
stream, turn left on to
another forestry track
(grid ref NN332261) which
leads back to the railway bridge,
where you retrace
your steps. Because of the
stream crossings, it is better
to use just the return half of the
walk in winter or after heavy
rain.*
Map: *Ordnance Survey
Landranger 50,
Harvey Superwalker Crianlarich.*

"This is the most beautiful pine forest
you will ever have the pleasure of
exploring. I guarantee it."

Before you go...

Listen out!

Les Borg

Listen for signs of the capercaillie when you're walking through woodland. Weighing in at up to 5.5kg, this turkey-sized grouse is one of Britain's largest land birds. It's so rare – about 1,000 survive from the 20,000-strong capercaillie population of the 1970s – you're unlikely to catch even a glimpse. But you may be lucky enough to hear its call early in the day.

Don't make the mistake of thinking it will sound anything like a bird. The capercaillie's call is more like a cross between two sticks being hit together and the last of a sinkful of water gurgling down a plughole. Another clue comes from its name – derived from two Gaelic words, 'capul' and 'collie', meaning 'horse of the woods' – which may explain why some people describe its call as being like a horse's hooves pounding the ground. If you do hear a capercaillie, don't attempt to get any closer. The birds are easily disturbed, especially when feeding.

Walk the lot!

If you want to journey through the national park on foot, walk the West Highland Way. This is Scotland's first and most popular long-distance walk, stretching 95 miles from Milngavie, on the outskirts of Glasgow, to Fort William, and will take you about a week to complete. To find out more information call 01389 758216.

Get into the spirit of things

For centuries, the whisky trade has been a vital money-spinner in these parts, although the proceedings are rather less illicit nowadays. Follow our guide to malt-tasting in the southern highlands:

Inchmurrin finds its source in Loch Lomond, and is a light, dry malt that doesn't linger. From Loch Lomond Distillery (tel 01389 752781).

Glengoyne takes its water from the Distillery Burn in the Campsie Hills, to form a mellow, oaky tipple. From Land Brothers (tel 01360 550229).

Deanston is a refreshing malt, bottled at 12, 17 and 25 years with a smooth, fruity taste. From Burn Stewart Distillers (tel 01786 841422).

Blair Athol has a hint of citrus, bottled at 12 years for a lingering flavour. From Blair Athol Distillery (tel 01796 472161).

Old Rhosdhu isn't actually very old at all. Bottled at five years, it is a light, clean malt from Loch Lomond Distillery (tel 01389 752781).

Information

The National Park Gateway Centre in Balloch should be your first stop for information – call 01389 772199.

For tourist information on the area, visit the website at www.visitscottishheartlands.org
For details of the national park, visit www.justoutstanding.co.uk
You'll also find plenty of route ideas at www.walkingwild.com

To get local advice on where to walk, call the relevant tourist information centre:
Aberfoyle tel 0870 720 0604
Ardgartan tel 0870 720 0606
Balloch tel 0870 720 0607
Callander tel 0870 720 0628
Drymen tel 0870 720 0611

Dunoon tel 0870 720 0629
Killin tel 0870 720 0627
Tarbet tel 0870 720 0623
Tyndrum tel 0870 720 0626

Stay here.
Country Walking stayed with John and Julia Cross in Easter Drumquhassle Farm, Drymen. Just inside the southern border of the national park and on the West Highland Way, it makes a great base for walkers, who will appreciate the hearty breakfasts.

For details call 01360 660893.

For details of other accommodation, call 0870 720 0629 and request the area/accommodation guide.

Walkers' rights of way

Thanks to a legislative blunder, rights of way are not shown on Ordnance Survey maps of Scotland. They show plenty of paths and tracks, but these aren't necessarily rights of way. But don't panic! This is how you can plan where to walk:

• Invest in a good guidebook. This will show many paths that, while clearly visible on the ground, aren't on the maps.

• Call the tourist information centre nearest to your chosen walk. They can advise you on possible routes and local conditions.

• It's also advisable to call the ranger service, particularly if you are planning an upland route. A national park ranger will advise you on where to walk. For the west of the park, including the Cowal peninsula, call 01301 702785. For the rest of the park, call 01877 382034.

• The Scottish Rights of Way and Access Society (Scotways) can tell you what is, and, just as importantly, what isn't a right of way in the area you are walking. For advice, call 0131 558 1222.

• The stag stalking season can affect access between August and October. There is a Hillphones service, backed by the Mountaineering Council of Scotland, for the Glen Dochart and Glen Lochay area – call 01567 820886 for recorded information on where stalking is taking place. Tourist information centres should also know where shooting is scheduled. If you really don't want to run into a shoot, get a copy of Heading for the Scottish Hills, published by the Scottish Mountaineering Trust (ISBN 0-907521-24-X). This has comprehensive contact details of estates active in the stalking season, so you can phone and check when the guns will be firing. It is available from the Mountaineering Council of Scotland, tel 01738 638227.

• Unless you know the area well, leave your faithful hound at home. Many farmers request that dogs do not cross their land, particularly during the lambing season.

• Although there is a law of trespass in Scotland, there is also a long tradition of access to wild places. Landowners are generally happy to allow access to walkers, as long as you act responsibly and follow the Countryside Code.

Did you know?

Astound your fellow walkers with these facts about Loch Lomond and the Trossachs:

The powan, a freshwater herring, is found only in Loch Lomond and Loch Eck, after being trapped since the Ice Age.

Loch Lomond is the largest area of fresh water in the British Isles.

There is a colony of wallabies on one of the islands on Loch Lomond.

The term 'the Trossachs' means 'bristly place'.

The Lake of Menteith is the only 'lake' in Scotland. A Dutch map maker misheard the word 'laigh', which means low-lying ground.

Highlands & islands

They are breathtakingly beautiful, wild and tempestuous, and at times so enchanting they make you feel giddy. It must be love...

Words: **Perry Cleveland-Peck, Morag Fleming and Peter Jackson.** Pictures: **Tom Bailey**

In the spring of 1786, the Scottish poet Robbie Burns wrote a song
– The Highland Lassie, O – about his sweetheart Mary Campbell. Sadly, the girl was "seized with a fever" and died later that year, but there are some who maintain the pair exchanged bibles and possibly some matrimonial vows before they were parted forever.

Country Walking also has a Scottish sweetheart – the Highlands and islands themselves. Such is our passion for the area, it may appear to some that we too are wedded to a piece of Scotland. To celebrate this marriage of sorts, we bring you four west-coast walking locations all on a matrimonial theme – something old, something new, something borrowed, something blue.

Our 'something old' walk is on the Knoydart peninsula. With just one road that stops well short of the peninsula, Knoydart is truly Scotland's last-known wilderness, as old as Heaven and Hell themselves, and sandwiched in between. Quite literally.

We've gone a little over the top with our 'something new', bringing you two of the latest long-distance paths to cross the Highlands and islands – the Coastal Way on Arran, and The Great Glen Way from Fort William to Inverness.

As for 'something borrowed' we've headed to the Isle of Skye, traditionally associated with climbing, and pinched back a couple of trails from the mountaineers. You too can walk in the Cuillin Hills or on the Trotternish ridge.

'Something blue' is more emotional, and concerns the seas and the skies. It is these two elemental forces that have carved out this breathtaking landscape, and, of course, you will no doubt feel blue in your heart when you once again have to say goodbye to this special place and head home.

Knoydart Peninsula

The signposts on Knoydart tickle me. As you leave the comfort of the forest, with its well-made paths, and head for the hills, there is a sign warning you of the dangers ahead. Think 'Abandon hope all ye who enter here' and you'll get the idea. If you ignore it and continue, you'll come across another sign indicating the road to Hell itself. Quite

> "We're not walking all the way from Heaven to Hell today – it would be a steep climb of eight or nine miles, and then we'd have to walk back."

literally. You see the lochs that sandwich the Knoydart Peninsula, Loch Nevis and Loch Hourn, translate as 'Loch of Heaven' and 'Loch of Hell' respectively. Undaunted, we brave the treacherous landscape, stopping only short of Hell itself.

Our walk starts in Inverie, with the track heading up into woods behind the village. My companions, Bob and Sam, and I stop frequently (a relief, actually, as the gradient is quite steep) to admire the nature teeming from the wood. The rhododendron tunnel is atmospheric and the wee robins that pop out to say hello are cute, and tame. Frondy trees are straight out of a fairytale, while the burns tumbling down the hillside are flanked by fluorescent green moss. All woods are compared to Tolkien's these days, but in this case it is justified.

At a decent height I remember to turn around to look at the view over the sea loch beneath. It's astounding, as the water glistens between the banks of Loch Nevis, which stretch out towards the ocean beyond. A shade more pastel is the Isle of Skye, past the point to the right, and when clear, like today, the jagged Cuillin ridge can be seen behind the southern tip of the island. Straight ahead, looking deceptively close, lies the mountainous island of Rum.

Knoydart sunset – evening falls on the beach at Inverie.

We're soon through the forest, with the formidable moorland outside. Well, the signpost tells us it's formidable. I'm paraphrasing slightly, but the sign tells us in no uncertain terms that the way beyond is rough, hard and dangerous, and if we are not properly equipped we should go home to our beds 'cos there is no help for 20 miles and if Mountain Rescue have to come out we'll be sorry'.

Well, fair enough, because beyond where we are headed there are four Munros, and this is the most remote area of mainland Scotland. Known as garbh chiochan – 'the rough bounds' – it is pretty accurate. As soon as you step off the path things

become hard going, with tussocky grass hiding ankle-wrenching boulders, bottomless bogs and even an underground stream. One of the more rugged and experienced of our party is heard to describe it as 'intolerable' and 'unacceptable' – tough words from him indeed, take it from me.

Luckily for us we are walking on the stalkers' path, a well-trodden track that is perfectly acceptable thank you very much. Travelling up the path we're heading into the mountains, towards a pass (Mam Barrisdale) with Luinne Bheinn ('Loo-ne-vin') – one of those Munros – looming up to the right of it. Impressive. Behind us we can see over Loch Nevis, or 'Heaven', and you can see why. But we leave Heaven behind us for now and press on...towards Hell.

We're not walking all the way from Heaven to Hell today - it would be a steep climb of eight or nine miles, and then we'd have to walk back– but we do have the pleasure of coming across a signpost pointing to Loch Hourn. The road to Hell is clearly marked!

Suddenly the path plunges us into a deep, dark wood which seems to have the disturbing effect of making our companion, Bob, considerably up his output of bad jokes and dodgy puns. Emerging, groaning, from the evil wood, we meet the guardians of the road – Highland cows that block the path. But it is hard to take them seriously, with their eyes hidden behind mop heads and horns offset by cuddly shaggy coats.

The 'Heilan' Coos' seem to be the last of the obstacles in our way, and suddenly the trail is more pleasant. It leads us close to the river and makes for a prettier walk, with the water skipping over the stones and delicate bubbles glistening like pearls in the sun. Soon we come across the loch at the head of the glen and our outward journey is almost at an end. We stop for a while and sit by the water in the sun, then wander up the length of the loch at our leisure.

As the light starts to fade we head back the way we came, resisting the temptation to bury Bob in the Forest of Bad Jokes, gasping in awe at the sunset over Rum, Skye and Loch Nevis, and congratulating ourselves on choosing a walk that finishes at the pub.

Some of the Inverie locals can be a little inquisitive.

Loch Hourn – Loch of Heaven'.

The Route

Inverie

Distance: *13km/8 miles.*
Time: *3 to 4 hours.*
Terrain: *Forest and moorland track.*
Route: *From Inverie (grid ref NG7600) head north-west past houses, then turn right on to the forest track. Emerge at the other end of the wood on a good stalkers' path (NM776998) heading south-east with trees on the right and hill on the left. Continue on this path, bearing north east below monument until Loch an Dubh-Lochain. Return by outward route.*
Map: *Ordnance Survey Explorer 413, Landranger 33.*

Isle of Skye

Get off the tourist trail
by heading to the top of
'The Misty Isle'.

Skye has been described as 'The Misty Isle' and for those who know the place, this sobriquet can be an understatement – we here at Country Walking know people who have been there on several occasions and are still to see the jagged Cuillins ridge for which the island is famous – it being hidden in the brooding storm clouds.

Skye is also considered a mountaineers' paradise. Both the fearful Black and softer Red Cuillins, and the Trotternish range, offer hours of rocky challenges for even the most experienced climber.

Mountains or not, Skye certainly is an awe-inspiring location, a place where elemental forces still rule the roost and man struggles to make his mark – trees have little chance here. Bleak, rugged and windswept, Skye is a place carved out by the sea and the wind, a location that we enjoy just as long as it lets us.

With this in mind, some walkers may think Skye has little to offer, preferring to seek out more pastoral locations on the mainland that provide easy walking and scenic views. Well think again, because Skye can provide some truly inspiring trails for walkers of all ages and abilities.

Photographer Tom and I meet Colin Simpson, of Scotland's Walking Wild tourism initiative, for a low-level route that takes us to a hidden place beneath a collection of pinnacles known as the Quiraing. The pinnacles are reminiscent of Skye's Old Man of Storr, a lonely, elongated teardrop-shaped rock on the east coast that, perhaps more than any other natural feature on this island, symbolises what Skye is all about – it's found on many a postcard. Here at the Quiraing, though, we have many more pinnacles to admire – handfuls of fingers of rock that stretch skyward in some unknown eternal plea, formed by massive landslips in the layers of basalt rock of which the area is composed.

Colin advises us to meet at a car park on the ridge above Loch Leum na Luirginn. When we arrive, the reason why is obvious.

Whereas from the coast road the Quiraing rises from on outcrop high above you, from Colin's car park the Quiraing meets you eye to eye. A gentle moorland footpath stretches off to the pinnacles ahead, hugging contours low down on the flanks of Meall na Suiramach all the way.

The Quiraing is part of the Trotternish range that stretches north-south from almost the very top of Skye to Portree, the island's main community halfway down, taking in the Old Man of Storr and the Storr group of ridges and pinnacles. The fact that the Quiraing sits at almost the most northerly point of the island – considerably further from the main ferry terminal than, say, the Cuillins – means the area is left largely untouched by visitors.

The Needle, with The Prison behind, is reward enough, and a picnic here against one of the many smaller boulders makes for a perfect denouement to any walk.

More adventurous walkers, however, can head up the slope for a space around the back of The Needle. Head around the left of the base and you reach a grassy hollow, offering impressive views over the top of The Prison and to the Trotternish range beyond. From here follow a path up between two pinnacles for the third of the Quiraing's surprises, The Table. You can reach the top of this large, flat, grassy area by a steep slope. It's a great spot for lunch – how often do you eat at a table outdoors? But food is not absolutely necessary. Just drink in the views.

A Highland cow embellishes a rare clear view of the Cuillin

Admiring the views over the Trotternish ridge

We set out from the car park and soon pick up a springy heather and moss path that dips in and out of the hillside folds. The path climbs gently, with the occasional encroaching rock to navigate around and perhaps one or two craggy burns to ford, but not what you'd consider in any way taxing (this may not be the case in winter, when the trail takes on a more boggy character). All the while, the strange formations get closer.

The Quiraing is a natural maze of pinnacles and escarpments, offering beguiling half-glimpses of the seas to the east and the Trotternish hills as they snake away southwards. On the southerly side of this breathtaking rocky amphitheatre, to the right as you head in, stands a formation known as The Prison, a sheer cliff with what looks like two sides of a forbidding castle keep or ancient fortress at its top. I can't help thinking that if I'd been found guilty of some unsavoury misdemeanour, I'd be more than happy to be locked up here.

Our path reaches the base of the Quiraing, The Prison rising up in front of us. We twist our way through the grey and orange lichen-clad boulders and find ourselves looking up at the next wonder of this labyrinthine place. Pointing to the sky is The Needle, a finger of basalt that rises heavenwards like some cocky earth-hewn insult to any disrespectful human being. For many, this view of

The Route

The Quiraing

Distance: *5km/3 miles.*
Time: *2 hours.*
Terrain: *Mud track, some grassy slopes.*
Route: *From car park (grid ref NG439679) cross road and pick up path heading north east to Quiraing. Return via same route. Under no circumstance should you try to reach the top of Meall na Suiramach from the Quiraing.*
Map: *Ordnance Survey Explorer 408, Landranger 23. Harvey Maps Skye Storr & Trotternish.*

Glen Coe

Walk in Scotland's infamous Valley of the Shadow of Death

"Charles Dickens commented, 'Glen Coe is perfectly terrible – it resembled a burial ground for a race of giants'."

The Route

Glen Coe's Lost Valley
Distance: *3.5km/21/4 miles.*
Time: *2 to 3 hours.*
Terrain: *Mostly steep moorland.*
Route: *From car park (grid ref NN171569) on A82 head down to old road near the river and turn left along it. Wooden steps lead down to a bridge over the river. Cross the rocks on the other side to join the path that rises steeply between Beinn Fhada and Gearr Aonach, the easterly two of the three sisters of Glen Coe. The path is clear, even when it crosses the deer fence and the burn. Coming up over the final rise, the valley stretches to buttresses leading up to Bidean nam Bean. Return by the same route.*
Map: *Ordnance Survey Explorer 384, Landranger 41. Harvey Superwalker Glen Coe.*

No visit to Scotland's west coast is complete without a walk in Glen Coe. It was here, in February 1692, that the Campbells massacred the MacDonalds of Glen Coe, and to this day the magnificent landscape has a tragic air about it. When Charles Dickens travelled through the valley in 1841 he commented, "Glen Coe is perfectly terrible – it resembled a burial ground for a race of giants."

Today the giants and Highland clans have disappeared, and the area is now home to walkers, climbers and even TV entertainers (Jimmy Savile has a house here). Glen Coe is a perfectly wonderful place to stretch your legs.

A road snakes along the valley floor, with many a parking spot to start and begin your walk from. We suggest you try our Lost Valley walk, where the MacDonalds were said to hide the cattle they had rustled from their neighbours.

Great Glen Way

Take a week off work and follow this new long-distance trail through the heart of the Highlands.

The Great Glen Way is Scotland's newest long-distance walk. Officially opened in 2002, this 73-mile route links Fort William, the gateway to the Western Highlands, with the beautiful city of Inverness. Through some creative navigation, the new trail also links into the 95-mile West Highland Way at Fort William, while at its other end, Inverness has an easy link to the Speyside Way, which leads to the Rob Roy Way that in turn meets the West Highland Way at Drymen. The result is an almost circular walking route of 331 miles through some of the finest scenery Scotland has to offer.

But it's one step at a time for me and my two walking companions, Alan and Alistair. And our first step is at the start of the Great Glen Way, at what remains of the old fort beside Loch Linnhe. We've walked a couple of long-distance trails before together, and we're going to do this one in style, planning each day's walking around our bed and breakfast stops along the route.

In its early stages the route skirts Loch Linnhe to join the Caledonian Canal at Corpach, where there are pretty lock-keepers' cottages and a 'pepper-pot' lighthouse. We set ourselves a modest goal for our first day, with just 101/2 miles to cover before our B&B at Gairlochy. The route follows the Caledonian Canal, and what it lacks in altitude it makes up in interest. Impressive aqueducts carry water beneath the towpath and the historic swing bridge of Moy, each half of which has to be opened separately. Everything, however, is overshadowed by the views south east, where the Ben Nevis range forms a spectacular sight.

Day two is also on the level, with the 12 miles ahead between Gairlochy and South Laggan lying on the western shore of Loch Lochy. The going is easy, with a mixture of forest paths and Tarmac, and much of the trail is shared with the Great Glen Cycle Route. Two Munros tower above the forest path, Stron a'Choire Ghairbh and Maell na Teanga, and these should only be attempted by competent and well-equipped climbers. As we leave our forest track, the road is flanked on both sides by banks of gorse and broom. Their brilliant yellow flowers and strong 'coconut' scent will remain for me a lasting memory of the Way.

Blessed with bright weather as we set out on day three, our objective is Fort Augustus, 101/2 miles further on, at the foot of Loch Ness. With thoughts of monsters on our minds, it is man-made beasts of steam we have to thank for the disused trackbed of the railway that once ran alongside Loch Oich, linking Spean Bridge to Fort Augustus. Further on, the trackbed gives way to General Wade's military road, a tree-lined path beside the loch that proves to be one of the most peaceful stretches of the entire trail. Activity returns with the colourful locks of Cullochy and Kytra, which lead us into Fort Augustus.

Fort Augustus is a bonny wee village with a flight of five locks at its centre. We tarry awhile beside the canal, buying delicious pork pies from MacDougall the butcher. After coffee, we are on our way to Invermoriston, for the shortest stretch of our trail, our destination just eight miles away along the shores of Loch Ness.

Day four, and the steep climb from Invermoriston offers fine views over Loch Ness. But the one thing we don't see is the famous monster.

We've saved the longest stretch for last, and as we rise on day six there are 18 miles ahead of us to Inverness. The first couple of miles are beside the A82, before we climb steeply through conifers. Our vista opens on to moors, before the woods envelop us once again as we descend to Inverness and the end of The Great Glen Way.

The Route

Great Glen Way
Distance: *117km/73 miles.*
Time: *6 or 7 days.*
Terrain: *Forest roads, towpaths and country tracks. Some steep sections.*
Route: *Start at remains of old fort beside Loch Linnhe, Fort William, (grid ref NN120755), through Corpach, Gairlochy, Laggan, Fort Augustus, Invermoriston to Inverness. Waymarked throughout.*
Map: *Ordnance Survey Landrangers 41, 34 and 26. Harvey Maps Great Glen Way.*

Isle of Arran

See all of Scotland on this easy-to-reach west coast gem.

They say that to experience Arran is to experience Scotland in miniature. When we at Country Walking first heard this we thought, "Yeah, yeah…nice marketing line." But, in fact, the island does feel very much like a microcosm of the mainland.

To the north, wild glens and impressive, cloud-swathed, jagged mountains sweep the highland landscape, be-jewelled with a resident population of 4,000 red deer. Golden eagles and peregrines are masters of the skies, while otters have made the lochs and burns their home.

To the south, the landscape changes remarkably. Gentle rolling hills undulate around sleepy villages tucked in leafy hollows and grassy folds. Soft, sandy beaches and crystal-clear bays provide a peaceful place to walk and relax. This, dare I say it, could be the English home counties, but an England of times past.

You can now get a brand new perspective of this 'Scotland in Miniature' thanks to the opening of Arran's latest walkers' treat – The Coastal Way. Apparently, 130,000 steps is all it takes to enjoy this 79-mile coastal path, circumnavigating the island as it does and taking in its many moods and personalities. If you don't have time to walk every square yard of the diverse and multi-faceted Scottish mainland, you could do a lot worse than think about a five-day trip around Arran.

Whatever the length of a sea voyage – to Arran it is a mere 55 minutes – that act of taking a ship has a magically distancing effect on the daily concerns of mainland life. Today, the clear blue waters between Ardrossan on the mainland and the ferry terminal at Brodick, on Arran, are enough to draw an immediate metaphorical line between the working humdrum and the walking holiday. It's seven in the morning and I'm on the foredeck, coffee in hand and a salty breeze in my face. Beside us, a clever seagull works out that an easier flight across to the island is to the leeward side of our ship – incredibly it keeps it up all the way to Arran. Further off, the dorsal fins of a pod of dolphins slice through the Clyde waters.

At Brodick we meet our hosts for the day. Hugh McKerrell is a retired civil servant from Edinburgh, who lives on the island now and was instrumental in creating the new coastal path. Kerr Robertson is an Arran man through and through, who for many

The castle at Lochranza, one of Arran's most famous views.

"Whatever the length of a sea voyage – to Arran it is a mere 55 minutes – that act of taking a ship has a magically distancing effect on the daily concerns of mainland life."

We head away from the beach and around the back of the point. King's Cave is so named because it is said to be the place where Robert the Bruce came to meditate on how to beat the English in battle, and thought up the mantra, "If at first you don't succeed, try, try again," after watching a spider build its web.

From the cave we head under the impressive Drumadoon cliffs, created in a volcanic maelstrom more than 60 million years ago and now almost peppermint in colour from the lichen. A fallen fulmar spits at us as we walk past.

We're on the beach now, heading back to our starting point, the sand decorated with strange seaweeds, flotsam and jetsam, not a cloud in the blue skies. Hugh regales us with details of our walk to come – the impressive Fallen Rocks on Sannox's shoreline that crumbled from the cliffs in the 1600s; the castle at Lochranza on the north shore and nearby Coillemore Farm, where Robbie Burns was said to have met Mary Campbell; the Druid Standing Stone near Old Byre and the Auchengallon stone circle; tea and cake at The Coffee Pot in Whiting Bay. It all sounds like walking heaven. Better get on with it.

The Route

Arran's Coastal Way
Distance: *128km/79 miles.*
Time: *5 days.*
Terrain: *The continuous path includes some stretches of roadway, forest track, coastline and more mountainous terrain – one stretch has to be walked at low tide.*
Route: *The Coastal Way runs around Arran, easily walkable in nine stages. A waymarking system (yellow circle) is gradually being introduced.*
Map: *Ordnance Survey Explorers 361 and 362, Landranger 69. Harvey Maps Superwalker Arran.*

Left: Time out for some lunch, and to admire Arran's enchanting coastline.

Left: Hugh 'opens' Arran's new Coastal Way... to cheers from Perry!

years worked for the Forestry Commission on the island. Both have a twinkle in their eyes and an energy that belies their mature years – is there something in the air on Arran?

We park near Kilpatrick on Drumadoon Bay, on the west coast of the island. We're heading out to Drumadoon Point to admire the cliffs there and take in the famous King's Cave. As we walk between the sandy beach and the grassy, wildflower fields, photographer Tom spots a golden eagle, seemingly hanging on the off-shore breeze. For a spell-binding five minutes, we watch as the great bird is mobbed by a kestrel – it is only when the kestrel gets close that you appreciate just how large and impressive the eagle is.

Before you go...

Arran

Accomodation
There are plenty of B&Bs on Arran. We stayed on the mainland in Irvine, 20 minutes from the ferry terminal at Ardrossan. The Annfield House is a charming three-star hotel – a 'country house in town' – set on the banks of the River Irvine. It boasts nine bedrooms, all with en-suite bathroom facilities, a bar and a well-respected restaurant. The hotel is close to town and enjoys pleasant views over the gardens.

Annfield House Hotel
6 Castle Street, Irvine, Ayrshire KA12 8RJ.
Tel: 01294 278903.
Fax: 01294 278904.
www.annfieldhousehotel.co.uk

General information
Brodick tourist information centre
Brodick ferry terminal. Tel: 01770 303774

Ayrshire & Arran Tourist Board
www.ayrshire-arran.com
For more information on the Arran Coastal Way visit
www.ayrshire-arran.com

Getting there
Caledonian MacBrayne – for the ferry from Ardrossan on the Scottish mainland to Brodick, on Arran, visit www.calmac.co.uk which has timetables and a facility for booking on-line. It's best to book the ferry as soon as possible because it does get busy. You need to book both outbound and inbound journey. If you are taking a car on the ferry, you need to be at the ferry terminal 30 minutes prior to the departure time. For general enquiries and administration call 01475 650100.

Car hire on Arran
Those who don't wish to take a car across, or are unable to book a car on the ferry, can book a hire car, to be collected at the ferry terminal at Brodick. Try:
Arran Transport *on 01770 302121.*
Blackwaterfoot Garage *on 01770 860277.*
Whiting Bay Garage *on 01770 700345.*

Maps and guides
Ordnance Survey Landranger 69,
Explorers 361 and 362.

Harvey Maps Superwalker Arran.
Tel: 01786 841 202, www.harveymaps.co.uk

Isle of Arran Coastal Way Map and Guide by Hugh McKerell (ISBN 1-90429-301-6), available from bookshops on the island.

Knoydart

Accommodation
The Pier House *is a licensed restaurant with rooms – call 01687 462347 or visit its website at www.thepierhouseknoydart.com There is a range of self-catering accommodation in and around Inverie.*

Glaschoille Lodge, *owned by the Earl of Lindsay, sleeps 10 and throws in the use of a Landrover and a maid to clean the fireplaces – call 01333 360251.*

Drew Harris *lets three properties on the Kilchoan Estate. The farmhouse sleeps eight, the old dairy four and the bunkhouse six – call 01687 462724.*

The Knoydart Foundation *runs the hostel near the village. It sleeps up to 25 in bunkhouse-style accommodation – call 01687 462242.*

General information
www.road-to-the-isles.org.uk/knoydart.html
www.theoldforge.co.uk

Getting there
By ferry: *From Mallaig board the MV Western Isles ferry ('Brucie' to its pals). Tel: Bruce Watt, the ferry man, on 01687 462320, or visit www.knoydart-ferry.co.uk*

By boat: *You can also charter a boat. Try The Old Forge for four to eight passengers (01687 462267) or Iain Wilson for up to 11 people (01687 462844).*

Food and drink
The Pier House *is a licensed restaurant with top-class food and a laid-back atmosphere. For details call 01687 462347*

Tho Old Forge *serves food all day with all sorts of weird and wonderful things popping up on the menu – kangaroo springs to mind, as well as venison, salmon and other local delicacies. They do a mean coffee, too, although often these are bypassed for the guest ales and the good selection of whisky. Call 01687 462320 or visit www.theoldforge.co.uk*
If you are self-catering you must take all food and drink in with you on the boat from Mallaig (there are very few provisions on the peninsula, although the pub will sell milk and bread if they have enough). Most owners of self-catering accommodation will pick you up from the ferry, and ours came prepared with a tractor and trailer, knowing we would be loaded down with food for a week.

Maps
Ordnance Survey Landranger 33,
Explorers 398 and 413.

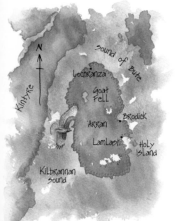

Annfield House Hotel – country house style in town

Ferries run between Ardrossan and Brodick

The Great Glen Way

Accommodation
There is a comprehensive accommodation list available on the Great Glen Way Website, www.greatglenway.com It's important to book early, and we used B&Bs throughout. Among the best were:

Dreamweavers
Earendil, Mucomir, By Spean Bridge PH34 4EQ. Tel: 01397 712 548

Bridgend House
The Green, Drumnadrochit, Inverness-shire IV63 6TX. Tel/fax: 01456 450 865.

*We also used the **Great Glen Baggage Transfer Service**. Tel: 01320 351 322 (mobile 07899 940955).*

Great Glen Way Ranger Service
Auchterawe, Fort Augustus, Inverness-shire PH32 4BT. Tel/fax: 01320 366 633. E-mail: greatglenway@highland.gov.uk www.greatglenway.com

Getting there
We used the Citylink coach, Edinburgh to Fort William and Inverness to Edinburgh. Tel: 0870 550 5050, www.citylink.co.uk

There are railway stations at both Fort William and Inverness. Tel: 08457 484950, www.railtrack.co.uk

Food and drink
There's a good choice in larger towns and villages along the route. Places worth looking out for include:

The Bothy *in Fort Augustus overlooks the canal and locks. Very good service and a great range of beers.*

Maps and guides
Ordnance Survey Landrangers 41, 34, 26 and 21, Explorers 399, 400 and 416.
Harvey Maps *publishes a Great Glen Way route map at 1:40,000. Tel: 01786 841 202, www.harveymaps.co.uk*

The Great Glen Way Rucksack Reader,
by Jacquetta Megarry, is indispensable. Tel: 01786 824696, www.rucsacs.com

Skye

Accommodation
We stayed at Blairdhus House, a beautifully situated four-star B&B with spectacular views over Loch Duich. All rooms are en-suite with TV, tea/coffee making facilities, radio, hairdryers and ironing facilities. Hearty breakfasts set up for your day's walking.

Blairdhu House
Kyle Farm Road, Kyleakin, Isle of Skye IV41 8PR Tel: 01599 534 760. www.blairdhuhouse.co.uk

Getting there
There is a toll bridge to Skye at Kyle of Lochalsh

General information
Portree tourist information centre
Bayfield Road, Portree. Tel: 01478 612137

Sky community website *www.skye.co.uk*

Maps
Ordnance Survey Landrangers 23 and 32, Explorers 407 to 412. Harvey Maps Skye The Cuillin, Skye Storr & Trotternish.

More information

Websites
Walking in the Highlands
www.walkingwild.com

Highlands of Scotland Tourism
www.host.co.uk

Visit Scotland
www.visitscotland.com

Tourist information
Cameron Square, Fort William. Tel: 01297 703781.

Weather forecasts
Glasgow Weather Centre.
Tel: 0141 248 3451.

Trains
We travelled to Fort William on Scotrail's Caledonian Sleeper. For more details visit www.scotrail.co.uk

After a fabulous walking break in Scotland, we returned to England with Great North Eastern Railway. For more details visit www.gner.co.uk